Radical Notes 7

THE FIRST GLOBAL ECONOMIC CRISIS OF THE 21ST CENTURY

Some Radical Perspectives

Edited by
Pratyush Chandra

The First Global Economic Crisis of the 21st Century:
Some Radical Perspectives
Edited by Pratyush Chandra

First Published, 2013

ISBN 978-93-5002-207-8

Published by
AAKAR BOOKS
28 E Pocket IV, Mayur Vihar Phase I, Delhi 110 091
Phone : 011 2279 5505 Telefax : 011 2279 5641
aakarbooks@gmail.com; www.aakarbooks.com

Printed at
Mudrak, 30 A Patparganj, Delhi 110 091

A movement in a sense is a struggle over the definition of reality—how reality is constituted. It is this struggle that builds the focus and targets of the movement, informing the praxes towards social transformation. Inherent in this struggle is the act of reclaiming—sense and sensibility, words and meaning...

The word "radical", which in this post-Cold War phase of Global Capitalism or globaloney has been reduced to a general notion characterizing all kinds of extremism and deviance, is one such word that has been time and again reclaimed by the practitioners of social transformation. "Radical" derived from the Latin word, 'radix' meaning 'root' = 'basic' = 'fundamental' is a concept that aptly defines a transformatory practice as an endeavour to reveal and target the essence of what is given to us in appearance. Radicalism in this sense is nothing but fundamental transformation rather than politicking in appearances. Further, and foremost, it is the all-round critique of the status quo and its genealogies, rather than accepting the disciplinary divide/boundaries that the capitalist system perpetuates in order to control labour-power and labour, our efforts and their fruits.

Radical Notes is an endeavour to coordinate the radical voices around the globe, with special focus on South Asia. In our view such focus (which could have been anything) is not just for convenience, given the facilitators' cultural and intellectual comfort, but is also needed to concretise any 'radical' pursuit. In our view South Asia provides us the opportunity to visualize the reproduction of 'global' capitalism and struggle against it in a regional setting. But we must remember such focus is always fluid with the ever-dynamic radical needs of the humanity.

Radical Notes booklets are contributions on social, cultural, political or economic issues from counter-hegemonic perspectives, which need not be confined to any established socialist and communist current of thought (though these approaches are most welcome).

Series Editors
Radical Notes

Preface

The Right, Left and Centre everywhere have proposed diagnoses and recipes to save the 'economy' from the deepening crisis, as if the economy in itself is something neutral, and we can struggle over its political colour once it is saved. Even when the system, i.e., capitalism, is blamed (taking into consideration the growing interest in Marx throughout the First World) for its own ailments, the revival is recommended—through various interventionist measures. There are many academic astrologers and quacks nowadays roaming and gossiping around irritating the capitalists—"we told you so". But the capitalist knows what to do. Yes, intervention, if it's must, but on whose cost—capital's or labour's? The capitalist must be bailed out, and the labourer must be reined in. Social corporatism is not at all bad, if it subjugates labour to the 'general interests' of the economy.

Capital doesn't want to mess up with labour. It has tried to evade the very circuit in which labour-power has to be bought in, but every time it does that destiny reminds it of its painful bond with labour. This time capital had almost created a world of its own without the nuisance of labour. But these consumers and debtors, on whom it relied so much, betrayed it—it suddenly realised that these were in fact the same little urchins—those children of labour, whose devilish smell and smile it wanted to forget.

Time and again, the capitalist class is reminded of the basic lesson in political economy that profit is ultimately generated through an engagement with labour. But this class which is composed of competing entities – individuals or groups –

relapses into amnesia once a level of prosperity sets in, as they compete to "accumulate, accumulate...." Ultimately, they all find it ideal to directly jump from M(oney) to M'(oney) without going through the strenuous process of production where they must deal with labour, which simply cannot behave like another dumb 'factor of production'.

Once capital comes to its senses, and realises its inevitable bond with labour, it tries very hard (and every means) to sterilize labour—alienating it from its creativity (hence, its destructivity) and thus, its humanity. Whoever—capital or labour—mobilises its class and community first during the crisis, commands the post-crisis phase. Here labour is always at a disadvantage, it has to make an enormous extra effort and prior preparation to come to command. If it arrives late, it gives enough time for capital and its agents to put themselves in their headquarters. They don't meet in the streets (only leaving their dogs and watchdogs for the street-fights) but in lavish boardrooms and in the offices of national and international agencies. The labouring multitude is reduced to its representatives, who are b(r)ought in these offices to negotiate a deal. Thus, a social compact under the command of capital is attained.

This is what has happened at various levels—at the industrial and governmental levels—through expensive bailouts, austerity and other policy measures that transfer the brunt of the crisis to the shoulders of the working class. Until and unless the working class realises that crisis too is a moment of class struggle, not of negotiation and compromise, and that class struggle never ceases whether in production or outside—in work or at the time of rest, and constructs its own solidarian praxis on the basis of this realisation, capital will continue to recompose it, i.e., the working class, so that it is complicit in its own exploitation. In fact, what is a compromise, but an institutionalisation of class struggle under the conditions of capital, in which the defeat of labour is immanent!

This volume refuses to provide a single homogeneous perspective on the crisis. It brings together various contributions that were published in Radical Notes at various junctures of the ongoing crisis. These articles represent a plurality (and, conflict) of stresses both at the level of analysing the crisis and of providing insights into diverse class strategies and their implications—indicating the various political economic tendencies that constitute the crisis—its expansion and dissipation. The complementarity of various perspectives may be grasped only in retrospect. However, one can at least admit that they provide a glimpse into the richness of radical (especially, Marxist) critiques of political economy.

Pratyush Chandra

Contents

1

How to Think About the Crisis

Michael Perelman

The Financial Crisis Goes Beyond Finance

The crisis today in mortgage lending does not come as a surprise to me. I discussed the build up to the crisis in a book published recently, *The Confiscation of American Prosperity.*[1]

The book describes more than three decades of concerted efforts to restructure the economy to respond to the anti-authoritarian spirit of the 1960s. Most important of all, the counterrevolution to the 60s was concerned about a decline in the rate of profits. The objective was to remake the United States as a capitalist's utopia with strict market discipline for ordinary people, while showing special favours on business. Tax cuts, deregulation, and a more business-friendly legal structure became the order of the day.

In this environment, the legal framework for union organization soon became unfriendly. Success showed up relatively quickly in the labour market, where capital halted the increase of wages by 1972—the year when real hourly wages peaked. Since then wages have oscillated but never again reached that level.

Profits began to recover, but on closer examination the recovery was unusual. In competitive industries, profits were not particularly high. Profits in producing goods concentrated in industries protected by intellectual property or government favouritism were better. But the big profits came in finance. Even major industrial firms, such as General Motors, Ford, or General Electric began relying on their financial divisions for much of their profits.

What was happening? According to the textbook model of economic growth, new productivity translates into higher wages, which, in turn, create more demand, which spurs industry to produce newer or better products, increasing productivity. In recent decades, debt rather than income spurred demand.

As profits recovered, more affluent people saw their portfolios increasing, creating what economists call the wealth effect: the increasing value of their stocks, and later of their houses, was treated as income, which generated demand. Frequently, people used their houses to borrow money to support this demand.

Production of physical goods was largely neglected. I am reminded of a conversation between Samuel Johnson and James Boswell, a quarter millennium ago. Boswell observed:

> Very little business appeared to be going forward in Lichfield. I found however two strange manufactures for so inland a place, sail-cloth and streamers for ships: and I observed them making some saddle-cloths, and dressing sheep skins: but upon the whole, the busy hand of industry seemed to be quite slackened. "Surely, Sir, (said I,) you are an idle set of people."
>
> "Sir (said Johnson) "We are a City of Philosophers: we work with our Heads, and make the Boobies of Birmingham work for us with their hands."[2]

Johnson, of course, was being ironic. The philosophers of the new economy were not. They breathlessly referred to a weightless economy.[3] Tom Peters, the management guru, derided old-line businesses as "Lumpy-object purveyors".[4] Even Alan Greenspan is fond of rhapsodizing about how modern production techniques are making the economy lighter and lighter:

> The world of 1948 was vastly different from the world of 1996. The American economy, more then than now, was viewed as the ultimate in technology and productivity in virtually all fields of

economic endeavor. The quintessential model of industrial might in those days was the array of vast, smoke-encased integrated steel mills in the Pittsburgh district and on the shores of Lake Michigan. Output was things, big physical things.

Virtually unimaginable a half century ago was the extent to which concepts and ideas would substitute for physical resources and human brawn in the production of goods and services. In 1948 radios were still being powered by vacuum tubes. Today, transistors deliver far higher quality with a mere fraction of the bulk. Fiber-optics has [sic] replaced huge tonnages of copper wire, and advances in architectural and engineering design have made possible the construction of buildings with much greater floor space but significantly less physical material than the buildings erected just after World War II. Accordingly, while the weight of current economic output is probably only modestly higher than it was a half century ago, value added, adjusted for price change, has risen well over threefold".[5]

Nobody seemed to sense that anything was awry. Leaders in the US were content to let the modern equivalent of the boobies of Manchester produce their goods in Asian sweatshops, and then borrow the proceeds from their masters to support their consumption.

The game depended upon continued growth, whether illusory or real. Deregulation helped to promote illusions of prosperity. So did the dot.com hysteria of the late 1990s. When the bubble burst, the Federal Reserve came to the rescue with low interest rates. Temporarily lacking sufficient confidence in the stock market, real estate seemed a better bet.

Real estate prices soared. People could borrow more on their houses. And with rapidly rising real estate prices, people could comfortably lend money to people who could not afford the loans because, after all, real estate would always increase in value.

To make the illusion even more solid, people believed that they could avoid risk. Ratings agencies told investors that paper based on this real estate was just a shade more risky than US government bonds..To seal the deal, investors sold "insurance," which promised to cover losses if the investment would go sour.

This insurance business was so brisk that the amount of

insurance sold was many times more than the face value of the investments. After all, selling this insurance was an easy way to profit from real estate market, which had nowhere to go but up.

When the music stopped playing, the regulators discovered that nobody was watching the store. Far more insurance was sold than the insurers could afford to cover. The ratings agencies are putting their seal of approval on the paper to get more fees.

The government just agreed to buy up bad debt to the tune of $700 billion, bailing out both crooks and incompetents. The government debt will give the neoliberals an excuse to cut more programmes to help needy people, while bailing out the rich.

Something similar happened a few decades ago with another war, a different Bush, and the same John McCain. Many years ago, Lyndon Johnson, who would have just celebrated his hundredth birthday, found himself stuck in a war he couldn't win. He also knew that if he raised taxes to pay for the war, the public would demand an immediate halt with a fury that he could not resist. Johnson relied on borrowing, which raised interest rates.

Savings and loan institutions, like the investment banks today, borrowed short and lent long. In this case, people put their savings in the banks and the banks lent out money on 30-year mortgages. To prevent gouging and make mortgages affordable, the savings and loans were prevented from paying interest rates high enough to keep depositors from exiting, which could leave them bankrupt.

The Reagan administration, including daddy Bush, moved to deregulate the savings and loans. Given this newfound freedom, crooks and nincompoops (including the current President Bush's younger brother) rushed in to take advantage of profiting from other people's money. As the scope of this disaster was becoming obvious, five senators, including John McCain along with Alan Greenspan (perhaps the Godfather of the recent financial crisis), rushed in to defend one of the more egregious Savings and Loan operations run by Charles Keating. Oh, yes, a small savings-and-loan in Arkansas, which was connected with Bill Clinton (who later allowed Congress to deregulate the current financial system, led by Senator Phil Gramm, John McCain's chief economic adviser) also ran into difficulties.

The savings-and-loan scam crashed leaving the government to pick up the pieces at a cost that is still debated, but which was still well over $100 billion—pocket change today.

The difference today is that our politicians now promise effective regulation this time around, just as they did with Sarbanes-Oxley in the wake of the Enron crash and the rest of the dot.com boom.

The Financial Side of the Financial Crisis

This crisis should be a teachable moment, but speculative excesses are a part of the DNA of capitalism. Leo Tolstoy began his epic novel, *Anna Karenina*, with the famous observation, "All happy families resemble one another, but each unhappy family is unhappy in its own way". Much the same can be said about depressions. Each depression seems unique and subject to as many interpretations as the most dysfunctional family. Hence what is unique to this crisis is the way that its build up departs from the general textbook model. Also, as I mentioned above, the other defining characteristic of this crisis is that debt rather than income spurred demand.

Financial assets demand a different treatment. Capital reacts with horror when wages increase, demanding the Federal Reserve to slam on the brakes. In contrast, soaring prices of financial assets are presumed to be incontrovertible evidence of a healthy economy.

The increasing value of these assets spurs people to increase consumption, often taking on debt, confident that their assets will appreciate even more. As Mark Twain observed about an earlier Gilded Age: "Beautiful credit! The foundation of modern society... 'I wasn't worth a cent two years ago, and now I owe two millions of dollars'."

In 2000, when the excesses and frauds of Enron, World Com, and the dot.com boom came to light, financial markets shuddered. The Federal Reserve came to the rescue lowering interest rates, which reduced monthly mortgage payments, allowing people to buy more expensive housing.

Once housing prices begin to rise, housing becomes an investment as well as the source of shelter. In addition, people, who suffered losses during the dot.com bust, saw housing as a safer investment than the stock market. Housing then transmuted into personal ATM machines, allowing people to borrow freely on the rising value of their property.

Underlying this financial froth, something more ominous was occurring. Business refused to spend much for investment in productive activities. Again, the textbooks tell a different story. They teach that high profits translate into investment, which create jobs, spurring demand, and making the economy grow. Such was not the case this time around.

Earlier this year, the British financial journalist, Martin Wolf, observed:

> The US itself looks almost like a giant hedge fund. The profits of financial companies jumped from below 5 per cent of total corporate profits, after tax, in 1982 to 41 per cent in 2007."[6]

This estimate is probably too conservative because many non-financial companies increasingly depend upon finance. General Electric, and in their more prosperous years, Ford and General Motors, largely depended upon finance. Retail companies offer credit cards in effect, selling insurance on their products in the form of extended warranties.

The US Department of Commerce reported that in 1992 about a third of all workers employed in US manufacturing industries were actually doing service-type jobs (e.g. in finance, purchasing, marketing, and administration). Updating this work, needless to say, has not been a high priority for government agencies.

Corporations also spend mind-boggling quantities of money just to purchase their own stock. After all, increasing stock prices boost executives' bonuses. For years, Exxon has been spending more money for stock buybacks than capital expenditures, all the while whining that the company needs more incentives to drill for oil.

What investment does occur is largely financed by depreciation allowances rather than previous profits. John Bellamy Foster offers an important measure of this reluctance to invest:

> Nine out of the ten years with the lowest net non-residential fixed investment as a percent of GDP over the last half century (up through 2006) were in the 1990s and 2000s. Between 1986 and 2006, in only one year—2000, just before the stock market crash-did the percent of GDP represented by net private non-residential fixed investment reach the average for 1960-79 (4.2 per cent). This failure to invest is clearly not due to a lack of investment-seeking surplus. One indicator of this is that corporations are now sitting on a mountain of cash—in excess of $600 billion in corporate savings that have built up at the same time that investment has been declining due to a lack of profitable outlets."[7]

Finance is attractive for another reason: it employs relatively few people. The intriguingly-named FIRE sector, which includes finance, investment, and real estate, employs only about 8 per cent of the private labour force. So, 8 per cent of the workers generate 41 per cent of the profits. Massive investments in information processing make such results possible.

Of the investment that does appear, finance may represent a disproportionate share. The government does not have recent data on types of investment by industry. The data do show that investment on information processing and software is about 37 per cent greater than investment in industrial equipment and manufacturing equipment. Of course, information processing is also important in manufacturing, but the data is suggestive.

Where Did The Money Go and Will Jobs Also Disappear?

On Monday, September 29 the stock market lost more than $1 trillion, about as much money as the Gross Domestic Product for an entire month. The next day, two thirds of the value suddenly reappeared. Yet, for the most part the tumult left most people unaffected, at least for the moment. More important, will the evaporation of all this wealth affect ordinary people?

Karl Marx's concept of fictitious capital is very useful in understanding these wild swings. I have explored this subject in more detail in an earlier book, entitled *Marx's Crises Theory: Scarcity, Labor, and Finance*.[8]

For Marx, capitalism uses markets to distribute labour into productive activities, but it does so very imperfectly. Part of the problem is that lack of knowledge about the future causes imperfect investments. These imperfections magnify as the economy seems to prosper making people become giddy about their chances of success.

Crises are capitalism's way of purging unproductive investments. In this way, crises eventually make the economy stronger, unless they become so severe that they shatter the foundation of capitalism.

The crises will become more violent if the distribution of income becomes too lopsided, leaving investors flush with money, while consumers are relatively strapped. Massive amounts of money will flow into speculative ventures, creating bubbles. In effect, a market which is supposed to be a wonderful feedback system to inform capitalists about the needs of society, takes on a perverse logic of its own.

Eventually, the bubble pops and there is hell to pay. The question today is how extreme this shock will be. Capitalism has shown considerable resilience in the past. What is happening now could turn out to be relatively mild or could be severe.

I use San Francisco as an analogy for my students. There will eventually be a serious earthquake that will do enormous damage. Nobody can predict what will happen. Even when the earth begins to tremble, the severity of the event may be in doubt.

Wall Street uses a somewhat related term, leverage, to describe the ability to magnify potential profits by investing borrowed money. When the economy begins leveraging, business borrows money to invest—not necessarily in productive assets. Leveraging can continue as long as people feel confident enough to finance these investments.

The government's modest limits on leverage have been systematically weakened, to the point where investment banks would be putting up as little as 3 cents, and even less, for each dollar invested. The riskiness of such practice should be obvious. A mere 3 per cent drop in the investment would wipe out the bank's own share of the investment.

The Federal Reserve also promoted increased leverage by holding interest rates low. Other regulators also paved the way for more leverage. Companies that choose the path of lower profits and lower risks are written off as stodgy and old-fashioned. Their stocks will flounder, reducing executives' bonuses. So, Wall Street investors willingly increased their leverage and risk. After all, investors prefer companies with high profits. Few are willing to take the time or have the expertise to understand the risks that might make profits appear high.

In Wall Street-talk, increasing leverage works so long as investors maintain a balance between fear and greed. By fear, Wall Street means a reluctance to take on too much risk. Although Wall Street normally applauds greed, it associates excess greed with a foolhardy approach towards risk. During euphoric times when fear of risk subsides, people put money in ridiculous schemes.

In his delightful book, Charles Mackay, related tales of shady operators bilking early investors a few centuries ago.

> One projector set up a company to profit from a wheel for perpetual motion. Another projector proposed "A company for carrying on an undertaking of great advantage, but nobody to know what it is." "Next morning, at nine o'clock, this great man opened an office in Cornhill. Crowds of people beset his door, and when be shut up at three o'clock, he found that no less than one thousand shares had been subscribed for, and the deposits paid. He was thus, in five hours, the winner of 2000 pounds. He set off the same evening for the Continent. He was never heard of again."[9]

The newfound wealth during times of growing leverage can create more demand, which can increase jobs and wages. As noted previously, such has not been the case. Speculative wealth has not produced growth in wages for ordinary people or any significant growth in jobs. In fact, cutting jobs to increase profits has been a major factor in sustaining the boom. A few years ago, the business press praised this practice as financial engineering, as if it were providing a productive service.

One factor that contributed to the lopsided economic growth

without jobs, which characterized the recent decades, is the practice of leveraged buyouts. Private equity companies, as they are known, buy up other companies using borrowed money, often based on the assets of the target companies. The takeover artists claim that they can create managerial efficiencies, making their takeover look attractive to potential investors. In reality, they charge their targets exorbitant fees, often paid for by debt that the companies must eventually pay back. Then, to cover this burden, the companies must cut both wages and jobs, as well as looting significant value from pension plans. Private equity businesses then turn around and sell these supposedly rejuvenated, but actually hobbled companies to an unsuspecting public, which fail to see the similarity between such investments and the perpetual motion machine that Mackay described.

In describing the necessity of a bailout for finance, the alarmists, who are not necessarily wrong, point to the job losses associated with the corporate restructurings that will follow bankruptcies. But these restructurings have been going on for decades. The bailout, however, is intended to facilitate a continuation of the destructive financial practices, which have also caused significant hardship to labour.

Obviously, a collapse will also harm workers and other ordinary people, but in the wake of a collapse the country will stand a better chance to restore some sanity to the economy.

Conclusion: Capitalism 101 (A Foundational Course)

Capitalism is the most efficient system known to mankind. Central to this efficiency is the supposed ability of markets to channel capital where it is most effective. The current financial crisis might be expected to throw some doubts on this dogma, but I do not expect that to be the case.

For example, in 2001, in the wake of dot.com bubble, the *New York Times* reported on one of the many excesses of the period:

> In the last two years, 100 million miles of optical fiber—more than enough to reach the sun—were laid around the world as companies spent $35 billion to build Internet-inspired communications networks. But after a string of corporate

> bankruptcies, fears are spreading that it will be many years before these grandiose systems are ever fully used.[10]

As mentioned earlier, the response was not to rethink the system, but to double down lowering interest rates to re-ignite the stock market. Investors, the government, and even ordinary people applauded the decision of Federal Reserve Chairman Greenspan, who appeared to be the wisest man in the universe at the time.

Greenspan's manipulation of the interest rate appeared to be so beneficial, because it occurred without any direct effect on the proverbial taxpayer. Parenthetically, why is it that this taxpayer ranks so much higher in our concern relative to the workers who make everything possible?

In retrospect, Greenspan's policy provided the fuel that helped to make the current crisis more threatening. Just as the solution to the dot.com crisis produced the current crisis, the present bailout, if it works at all, will create the preconditions for the next one.

The purpose of the bailout is to create confidence. Back in the 19th century, the governor of Illinois gave an excellent analysis of the way confidence worked in financial markets. He said that confidence "could only exist when the bulk of the people were under a delusion. According to their views, if the banks owed five times as much as they were able to pay and yet if the whole people could be persuaded to believe this incredible falsehood that all were able to pay, this was 'confidence'."

His words may perhaps be the most succinct analysis of fictitious capital that I have read.

Now class, here is the question for all the students in Capitalism 101: explain to me how markets are so efficient in directing capital where it is most needed. Extra credit if you can do so without any giggles. (October, 2008)

REFERENCES

1. Michael Perelman, *The Confiscation of American Prosperity: From Right Wing Extremism and Economic Ideology to the Next Great Depression*, Palgrave Macmillan (2007).

2. James Boswell, *Life of Johnson*, 6 vols., Oxford University Press (1934-64).
3. Diane Coyle, *The Weightless World: Strategies for Managing the Digital Economy*, MIT Press (1998).
4. Tom Peters, *The Circle of Innovation: You Can't Shrink Your Way to Greatness*, Knopf (1997).
5. Alan Greenspan, *"Remarks" at the 80th Anniversary Awards Dinner of the Conference Board*, New York, October 16, 1996.
6. Martin Wolf, "Why it is So Hard to Keep the Financial Sector Caged", *Financial Times*, February 6, 2008.
7. John Bellamy Foster, "The Financialization of Capital and the Crisis", *Monthly Review*, April 2008.
8. Michael Perelman, *Marx's Crises Theory: Scarcity, Labor, and Finance*, Greenwood Press (1987).
9. Charles Mackay, *Extraordinary Popular Delusions and the Madness of Crowds* (1852)
10. Simon Romero, "Shining Future of Fiber Optics Loses Glimmer", *The New York Times*, June 18, 2001.

2

Fictitious Capital and Real Compacts

Anitra Nelson

Perhaps we need a Marxian to sort out the world's financial woes. The insights of Karl Marx on capitalist crises, especially speculation and financial crises, were sophisticated for his time. Indeed, this nineteenth century communist revolutionary called financial assets and loans 'fictitious capital' or 'imaginary wealth' as distinct from 'real capital'—industrial or productive capital—such as factories and commodity stocks.

The first part of this article discusses Marx's concepts of crises and fictitious capital in the current international financial climate. It relies on my doctoral study, which was published in 1999, *Marx's Concept of Money: The God of Commodities* (Routledge, London). Many contemporary commentators focus on what might be done to remedy the situation. Instead the second part starts from the premise that the current crisis illustrates the very destructive and inhumane nature of capitalism and argues for instituting a humane and ecologically sustainable world without money. This second part draws from my site—*Money Free Zone*.

Fictitious Capital

Marx stressed that stocks and shares are often exchanged at 'prices' at variance with the value of the real assets that they represent. In other words, financial capital circulates relatively autonomously of the productive process from which it arises and on which it depends, an endless tango, contributing to capitalist cycles and financial crises.

The current speculative boom in the USA has focused on housing investments. A pass-the-parcel style of lending evolved. Lenders were so cocky that borrowers would repay unabated, successive interests enthusiastically bought in down the line through mortgage-backed securities. This has led to a domino-like fall of credit once repayments seized up and as defaults rose. Hyman Minsky[1] has elaborated on this model of lending and its role in capitalist crises.

Repayments were jeopardised by wild lending practices, which meant that home loans were provided to many borrowers who had little hope of repaying. In a neo-conservative policy climate, it was assumed that the market, lending institutions, would price such loans for risk (through insurance). Though less severe than in the USA, in Australia lending was characterised by greater quantities and varieties of household credit (see Steve Keen's *Oz Debtwatch Site*). This kind of lending has strongly contributed to the current international financial crisis, in terms of over-speculation.

In *Capital III* Marx writes that when a sufficient proportion of capitalists invest, i.e. lend, without receiving repayments plus interest or profits, a generalised crisis will evolve of the dimensions we are now experiencing:

> If the reproduction process has reached the flourishing stage that precedes that of overexertion, commercial credit undergoes a very great expansion... the point when jobbers first enter the picture on a notable scale, operating without reserve capital or even without capital at all, i.e. completely on money credit... Interest now rises... It reaches its maximum again as soon as the new crisis breaks out, credit suddenly dries up, payments congeal, the reproduction process is paralysed and... there is an almost absolute lack of loan capital...[2]

With mortgage-backed securities both borrower and lender rely on the houses maintaining their value. Everything is inclined to tumble if either house prices fall or borrowers' incomes are threatened enough to compromise their ability to keep making loan repayments. In fact, defaults and falling prices tend to stimulate one another, setting up a negative dynamic. This has happened in New Zealand, Australia, the USA and the UK.

Capital: Money Begetting More Money

Basically, all investment lays bets on future returns. Investment is always a gamble. Indeed the rationale for capitalists' making profits is embedded in return for risk. If the risk doesn't pay off, they lose their money. So be it. Of course, this accepted reward for risk is turned on its head if those responsible for over-lending are 'bailed-out' by the US and so many other, including Australian, governments.

In Marx's time similar dilemmas raised the same quibbles:

> "...where the entire interconnection of the reproduction process rests on credit, a crisis must evidently break out if credit is suddenly withdrawn and only cash payment is accepted, in the form of a violent scramble for means of payment. At first glance, therefore, the entire crisis presents itself as simply a credit and monetary crisis... On top of this, however, a tremendous number of... purely fraudulent deals, which now come to light and explode; as well as unsuccessful speculations conducted with borrowed capital... It is clear that this entire artificial system of forced expansion of the reproduction process cannot be cured by now allowing one bank, e.g. the Bank of England, to give all the swindlers the capital they lack in paper money... Moreover, everything here appears upside down, since in this paper world the real price and its real elements are nowhere to be seen... This distortion is particularly evident in centres such as London, where the monetary business of an entire country is concentrated...".[3]

Today, of course, we have an international economy and one of the prime financial centres in question is Wall Street, New York.

However, as Marx stressed, the irony of the ideal of the individual in capitalism is in the omnipotence of the economic system over capitalists and workers and the dependence of our whole society and politics on growth. Thus we cannot afford to let the swindlers go to hell, because they will drag us there with them (while we cling to capitalism).

Material Bases for Crises

For Marx, economic crises were endemic and exogenous features of capitalism, which occurred at any time of substantial or widespread interruption to the production or circulation of commodities. Because capitalists act independently, indeed competitively, the result is a constant tendency to crises. Demand and supply is unorganised at every level (individual firms, particular sectors and national capital) and there is the constant necessity for generalised growth, based on profits (invested capital), which might not eventuate.

Thus the precarious material bases of capitalism sensitised the system to crises resulting from imbalances of demand and supply between different sectors of production, over-production or underconsumption (workers not being paid enough to buy the products they create) and speculation. Speculation or unwise investment appears after the fact in all these cases. At the same time, overinvestment—too many people wanting to invest and gain returns from the available capitalist activities—also leads to bubbles or boom. Then they burst or bust. So, while poor regulation or lack of regulation of lending institutions might exaggerate a crisis, no specific regulation of banks could avert the general and constant phenomenon of capitalist crises.

Today, too, many commentators are arguing that throwing money at Wall Street and lenders not only means throwing proverbial good money after bad but might not solve the problem because it is not *simply* a credit crisis. One argument has been that the 'bail out' must provide 'little' people with mortgage repayment support, not for reasons of social justice but because such support is critical in *material* terms to overcome the basis of the crisis. Home purchasers must be supported so they can keep repaying their mortgages and keep the lenders solvent. This way the crisis finds some floor, or safety net.

These arguments accord with Marx's materialist analysis, which was based on the exploitation of workers by investors, entrepreneurs and managers. Marx's materialism was centred in human behaviour; the economic categories of profits and growth were social creations dependent on slave-like deliverance of commodity and service-producing labour to capitalists. This system requires the constant ritual of work for monetary pay, money in a sense circulating effort, assets standing for past labour.

Rising House Prices

The last decade of burgeoning household debt in Australia has been accompanied by rising residential house prices. A mainstream analysis suggests too few houses and apartments, the need for government to open up and service more land and high-rise buildings in cities. This analysis fails to refer to inequities within our country, namely rising numbers of households that have two houses, such as families with holiday houses and a second house inhabited by student children.

Current mainstream analyses also tend to deflect attention from the most interesting aspect of the current lending boom —pushing up house prices, in effect incorporating speculation within ordinary households. In Australia, as house prices have risen to levels which have alarmed the International Monetary Fund, rents have increased strongly too.

Today, in Australia, paying for a home and superannuation complicates worker-employer relations. You could say that each worker has become a bit of a capitalist. Or, you could reason that workers not only get paid less than the value of the result of their work but also pay substantial proportions of their wages back to capitalists in the form of borrowing for larger and more expensive homes and by mandatory investments in superannuation.

Thus, workers are even more exploited in invisible or contradictory ways. Tenants link into the same structure—there is no escape. However, Marx was not the first to recognise that the game is one of mutual hostages. Around half the finance lent by Australian banks today goes to, and *comes from*, mortgagors. If they were alive now, the authors of the *Communist Manifesto*, Marx and Engels, might well rally: 'Borrowers of all countries unite...'[4]

Real Compacts (v. Fictitious Capital)

Part of the reason that I chose Marx's concept of money as the subject of a doctoral study related to my experiences as an activist, especially in the women's liberation and environmental movements, and reflection that the basic building block of the capitalist system is money. By the end of that study, which involved reading many people's ideas about what money was —and how it 'worked'!—I decided that the only way forward was to dispense with money altogether. Some of those thoughts were expressed in an article published in 2001—'The Poverty of Money: Marxian Insights foı Ecological Economists' (*Ecological Economics* 36, 499-511). Late last year I brought together my thoughts about experiences in cooperatives and with permaculture, and from reading and discussions on utopian and other literature at a site—*Money Free Zone*.

The Compact site calls for a 'compact' society. Compact means both 'an agreement' and 'small and efficient'. The argument is that money-free social relations, a 'compact society', will enable, embody and reproduce fairness, equity and sustainability. In a compact society our everyday practices will be modest and effective, minimising resource and energy use to meet simple and basic needs. We need to even out the inequalities between people within regions and between regions.

The idea is that formal collective agreements, compacts, will enable us to act in concert, to avoid some people's activities undermining other people's efforts. Networks of compacts will form the basis of compact neighbourhoods, compact communities, compact regions and a planetary compact society.

Visions and strategies for establishing sustainable practices proliferate but are in conflict with economic prerogatives that still dominate decision-making and actions. Capitalist practices are based on trade, exchanging goods and services for money, and producing goods and services for trade. The whole production process and decisions about how and what to produce are centred on the market.

This market logic uses monetary calculations. It is as if money is our common god, our central value, and provides the principles for all our main relationships and activities. Within this mainstream perspective, even sustainability initiatives must be 'economic', an example being the dominance of 'triple bottom line' approaches. Thus the world is still seen through capitalist eyes: fragmented in units in accordance with economic criteria and credentials, i.e. profitability.

Current sustainability initiatives are failing because really sustainable practices require that non-monetary values, principles and relations rule our decision-making and activities. To be sustainable we need to treat everything according to their use-value and use-value efficiencies, i.e. minimising needs and environmental impacts, and use-values must include ecological values.

Thus we must dispense with the market requirement of monetary values and calculations, i.e. capitalist determinations and complications, structuring business around assets and flows, credits and debits. Ecological processes and dynamics are hard enough to understand and manage without overlaying needs to make production and exchange sensible in terms of markets.

The concept of 'compact' is akin to 'contract' but involves none of the monetary values and financial risks common in contracts. Compacts have the potential to provide the political and economic building blocks of a world without monetary relations and values. Compacts would commonly involve at least two parties that agree, for instance, to share the use-rights and responsibilities of a resource base or to provide one another with goods and or services. In other words, compacts would express agreements over the use and management of resources necessary to enable people to exist modestly and to share responsibilities as stewards of the earth and all its natural communities.

Compacts and networks offer viable forms for people to take and share direct power. Compacts would encompass all kinds of activities, including collective production and spheres of exchange, organised locally and in local-to-local networks. Thus we refer to a 'compact movement' as networks of socially fair compacts between groups and individuals, compacts that respect environmental sustainability and that will merge to form a dynamic path to rational, humane and sustainable livelihoods.

Many people have some relationships and practices consistent with a vision of compact communities. A 'compact movement' is already apparent in individual acts and voluntary associations as people place humane and environmental principles and values above monetary, capitalist ones. Generalising such values and formalising them in compacts will create alternative forms of governance, ultimately a global compact society.

This vision is not wholly new: many liberation philosophies

point in the direction of a planetary compact society. Anarchism, permaculture, humanism and communism give priority to equity and fairness between people along with living in modest and sustainable ways, respecting nature. Associated principles and values have been expressed in the writings and actions of many philosophers and activists. However, a key distinction of the compact vision from numerous others is that production and exchange on the basis of people's and planetary (ecological) needs will take place without using money, or monetary values, principles and relationships.

Networks refer to the internal communications and relations between members within compacts as well as external connections comprising further compacts and other kinds of relations supporting compacts. For instance, a household would be organised by way of a compact which, in turn, would be a member of other compacts specifically formed to sustain the household and to help its members to sustain other people within their neighbourhood comprising people and the local natural and built environment.

Current capitalist practices contradict universal human rights to basic needs such as food, clothing, shelter, safety and care. Every activity involves monetary considerations at some level, shackling direct and sensible responses to human and environmental needs. Non-monetary compacts and networks would work directly with available human skills and effort, and energy and materials assessed in terms of their use-values.

Every human being would have a right to basic needs and would be a member of compacts designed to fulfil those needs at the same time as belonging to networks that would make them responsible for fulfilling other people's basic needs and care for the local environment. Planning and distribution formalised in compacts would be facilitated using electronic communication, which would link households with neighbourhood precincts and broader, sub-bioregional communities and bioregional networks.

Compacts and networks would be diverse, fulfilling a variety of purposes for numerous members. As basic ways of organising, formal compacts would offer robust and stable forms for local to global organisation of all kinds of activities, from those directed at fulfilling basic needs and wants to cultural and recreational ones. Permaculture and alternative, appropriate, technologies for generating energy and extracting and processing resources offer ready-made ways to proceed.

Some people would need to resettle according to the natural opportunities and limits of local and regional environments. Even so, place-based living would allow for mobility outside local groups, especially for members with skills and knowledge to share. Non-monetary exchange has always relied on customary rights and responsibilities with local and personal variations associated with social and environmental circumstances and developments. Non-monetary exchange will involve compacts and networks that allow groups to have access to basic needs and wants from outside the local area when necessary.

The deficiencies of local collective self-sufficiency and production for direct use-values can be overcome through low levels of exchange enabled by e-communication, negotiated on terms specific to the potential and limits of the people and landscape in question. Thus spheres of exchange would be minimal and formal and either of mutual advantage to two exchanging individuals or communities or involve multilateral benefits to many individuals or communities.

Strategies

The transition to a world without money—which is only to say that the conditions are laid for humans to establish communities based on social justice and environmental sustainability—would be created by, on the one hand, diminishing production and exchange based on a monetary, capitalist rationale and, on the other hand, progressively taking over production and exchange using non-monetary compacts. Collectively, our actions would weaken a reliance on capitalist practices and *strengthen* networks of compacts as alternative forms of governance, production and exchange.

Permaculture (permanent, sustainable agricultural practices and principles of designing sustainable livelihoods) offers ways to think about, plan, strategise and act to create a world that is socially just as well as environmentally sustainable. Permaculture emphasises self-reliance, production for direct use, minimising exchanges and concentrating them in the local area, working collectively and with nature rather than competitively and to control nature.

Monetary exchanges and production for the market must be re-modelled into exchanges that focus not only on the use-values of the produced and exchanged goods and services but also on the parties to such exchanges. Thus production and exchanges would be formally planned, centre on collective sufficiency based on bioregions managed for environmental sustainability and would involve production and exchange only marginally for identified, specific, external groups and environments.

Sustainability requires the end of the market, production for trade, and trade. Instead, we must care for the earth, care for people, and share the surplus.

(October, 2008)

NOTES

1. For more on Minsky and his financial instability hypothesis, see -http://cepa.newschool.edu/het/profiles/minsky.htm.
2. K. Marx (1981, orig. 1894) *Capital: A Critique of Political Economy* Volume III [David Fernbach translation] Penguin Books Harmondsworth: 619-20. [Chapter 30, if reading another edition].
3. Ibid: 621-22.
4. Following the final paragraph of K. Marx and F. Engels (1847-48) *The Manifesto of the Communist Party*, often referred to as *The Communist Manifesto*. In a recent Australian edition published by Ivy Press (Wingfield, South Australia) in their Manifesto Series with an introductory critique by David Boyle, this paragraph (70) reads:

   "The Communists disdain to conceal their views and aims. They openly declare that their ends can be attained only by the forcible overthrow of all existing social conditions. Let the ruling classes tremble at a communist revolution. The proletarians have nothing to lose but their chains. They have a world to win. Workers of All Countries, Unite!"

3

On the Character of the Current Economic Crisis

Spyros Lapatsioras, Leonidas Maroudas, Panayotis G. Michaelides, John Milios and D.P. Sotiropoulos

In the third chapter of *Capital*, Marx observed: "As long as the social character of labour appears as the money existence of the commodity and hence as a thing outside actual production, monetary crises, independent of real crises or as an intensification of them, are unavoidable. It is evident on the other hand that, as long as a bank's credit is not undermined, it can alleviate the panic in such cases by increasing its credit money, whereas it increases this panic by contracting credit" (Marx 1991: 649).

As we know, financial crises are sometimes the prelude to, and sometimes the result of, a crisis of over-accumulation of capital. Sometimes, again, the financial crisis manifests itself independently of the broader economic conjuncture, that is to say does not have any significant effect on the level of profitability and the level of employment of the "factors of production" in the other sectors of the economy above and beyond the financial sphere or some specific parts of it.[1] This, for example, is what happened in the case of the international financial crisis of 1987, when there was a collapse of share prices in the international stock exchanges, providing the international press with the opportunity to speak of a "return to 1929 and the Great Depression". But it is also what happened in most of the more than 124 crises in the banking system that were recorded between 1970 and 2007.

It is thus evident that each specific financial crisis must be examined both in relation to its particular characteristics and in relation to its interaction with other spheres of economic activity and the wider economic conjuncture, before it becomes possible to draw conclusions as to its causes, its extent and its consequences.

We shall argue that the current crisis is the outcome of permanent characteristics of capitalist relations of production and reproduction, but also of characteristics that are peculiar to the core of the neoliberal organisation of this relation, that is to say to the core of the present form of appearance of capitalist relations of production.

1. Factors in the Crisis

1.1 Some Basic Points from Marx

Marx showed in *Capital* that capitalism is not simply a system for extracting surplus labour or appropriating surplus product (the extraction of surplus labour and appropriation of surplus product are characteristics of *every* class society: the slave-owning society, the feudal, the Asiatic...). The distinguishing feature of capitalism is that *the process of generating surplus product takes the form of money producing more money as an end in itself*. In this context money is not a "produced commodity" as was believed by Classical Political Economy (and as is maintained even today in Ricardian readings of Marx) but the "reification of the capital relation".

Money is thus produced in accordance with the dynamics of expanded reproduction of the capital relation, first and foremost as credit money, as discounting of the future, as *the present portion of future profitability* and by extension *future income*. Thus, capitalism is "a system of production, where the entire continuity of the reproduction process rests upon credit" (MEW 25: 507. Marx-Internet 1894, Ch. 30). "This social character of capital is first promoted and wholly realised through the full development of the credit and banking system... The banking system shows, furthermore, by substituting various forms of circulating credit in place of money, that money is in reality nothing but a particular expression of the social character of labour and its products" (MEW 25: 620. Marx-Internet 1894, Ch. 36).

The financial system is thus a basic lever for expanded reproduction of overall social capital.

One essential element in the functioning of the financial system is "economic time", the difference between present and future value, that is to say the expectation of future profitability (of future returns) on which present discounting is dependent. *The tendency towards expansion of the monetary means that are called upon to function as capital in accordance with the expected future production and profit is an inherently unstable element of the system, a perennial potential for financial crisis.*

One significant component of present-day developments in the sphere of credit and finance, not unrelated to the breakdown in the system of fixed exchange rates and internationalisation and liberalisation of financial markets, is the development of financial derivatives. Through financial derivatives there is a mingling, a linkage and a comparison in profitabilities at the international level between every type of financial security. International capitalist competition is sharpened, with corresponding intensification of the international mobility of capital and the pressure imposed on labour for increased "international competitiveness".[2]

1.2 The Neoliberal Model for Regulation of Financing

Present-day developments in the financing process date from the beginning of the 1980s and have their origins in abolition of the restrictions that had been imposed after the crisis of 1929 on banks, the international movement of capital and the mode of operation of stock exchanges (particularly in London and the USA). In other words, they have their origins in the emergence of what is called the *neoliberal framework for regulation* of the financial sphere. We say regulation and we do not use the usual term "deregulation" because in the neoliberal model there is no abolition of regulation, nor in the final analysis of the guarantees provided by the collective capitalist (the state) for such functioning of the financial system as is right and proper for accumulation. The post-war "Keynesian" regulation (Bretton Woods) was merely replaced by a different kind of regulation that is compatible with the functions required by the neoliberal model of the financial system. A comprehensive framework of rules and regulations for the financial system is in operation today. For example, the functioning of the central banks as technical centres for underwriting the operations of the money markets and the credit system, is carried out through a broad mesh of regulations, rules and hierarchies, and the procedure for decision-making beyond the boundaries of democratic legitimacy in itself comprises a major systemic reform. Another example is Basel I and II as systems for regulating the behaviour of banks that are under the control of the central bank, etc.

The basic characteristic of the regulatory framework for the financial sphere—which is *a structural characteristic and core component of the neoliberal model*—is the development of extra-bank (i.e. non-traditional) financing of the public debt and enterprises by the international markets. The enterprises, at first large internationally active ones but with subsequent extension to medium-sized companies of suitable creditworthiness, finance their activities mostly through non-traditional sources of banking credit. They issue short-term commercial paper, sometimes using the stock exchange, sometimes resorting to a variety of non-bank financial arrangements (including insurance funds, mutual funds, hedge funds, insurance companies and a whole constellation of special forms of capital) entered into for this purpose. It is not only business companies that subsequently acquire access to non-bank financing and risk-management facilities but also those seeking housing loans, student loans, loans for the purchase of a car, credit cards, loans taken out by municipalities, etc.

This financing model presupposes securitisation of debt and international mobility of capital, that is to say *the bringing into existence of an international space of multiple investment spheres for individual and isolated capitals, a space whose functioning makes these prerequisites into expanded consequences*. The financial markets have developed into a complex multi-dimensional system. They are not just money markets, bond markets, share markets, currency markets and commodity markets. They also include a rights market and a market in fixed-income securities and every other kind of security. As a result, *an international of capital* has come into existence that is permanently on the lookout for secure profits and self-valorisation of money. Members of this International are combing the planet in search of reliable returns. Reliable returns in the sense that risk management (that is to say the probability of the expected return not being achieved) are the basic concern in an international market where multiple divergent forces are determining returns. It is a complex technique that prides itself on being a science.

From Marx we know that capitalist relations of production are engaged in expanded self-reproduction. *And the minimum element constituting that process is a claim to appropriation, a title of ownership of value and the terms of its production, a promised appropriation of surplus value. Securitisation of claims on future value and surplus value is thus unequivocally an element in the capital relation.* Its reproduction amounts to a perpetual production of securities and a perpetual endeavour to overcome resistances of the valorisation process, resistances that stem from "nature" and from labour: to overcome resistance in the potential spheres of utilisation and to overcome resistance to profitability created by other capitals. Risk management is incorporated into the production process precisely because there can be no assured outcome of any struggle against something that is resisting. What we see as risk management is therefore nothing other than the continuation by other means of the everyday class war against labour in the sphere of production, the continuation by other means of the everyday war between capitals whose aim is to secure the normal rate of profit in an international sphere of investment. Securities markets and risk management techniques have always been part of the same logic as the class power of capital and the wars that it wages.

The neoliberal model for financing capitalist production and reproduction played an important role in facilitating resurgence from the crisis of overaccumulation that made its appearance in the 1970s and continues to have an important function for capitalist accumulation and expanded reproduction.[3] The crisis had made its appearance at the beginning of the 1970s as a crisis of stagflation with increased unemployment and underemployment of the accumulated capital. The cause of these phenomena, i.e. the substantial outcome of the crisis of overaccumulation, was the fall in the rate of profit in the countries of developed capitalism that occurred in consequence of the overall pattern of social contradictions and antagonisms. These have rendered superfluous a section of the accumulated means of production.[4]

The functioning of the financial system and the means by which it is activated (for example the various forms of security) do not comprise merely vehicles for speculative investments. They are much more so components of a mechanism that makes a decisive contribution to the mobility of individual capitals, establishing the conditions for their competition. It thus functions as a key link in the reproduction of overall social capital. *Exposing individual capitals to international competition for financing of their activities makes it possible for there to be rapid reward of profitable, and punishment of insufficiently profitable, investments.*

This function has contributed, and continues to contribute, to transformation of banking activity because of the change in the correlation of forces between banks and the money market. More specifically, and as always in relation to our subject, the process of liberalisation of the financial system had significant consequences for the functioning of the banks, which may be summarised as follows:

(a) Bonds and shares are both securities. But, in order for them to be able to act as sources of finance for individuals or insurance funds or other non-traditional banking institutions, businesses or private citizens (for example with housing loans, etc.) *other forms of securitisation of debt must be developed*. Securitisation of debt has become an important process. It has contributed both to the emergence of the contemporary credit system and to its current crisis.

(b) The various non-bank financial schemes in operation on the international capital markets are not afflicted with the regulative restrictions that apply for banks, and are able to lend money at low rates of interest. This has had consequences for the functioning and the structure of the banking system. The new arrangements have squeezed bank profits and changed the composition of their workload, i.e. led to an increase in loans to households and loans to cover consumer and housing expenditures and a reduction in loans to businesses.

Consequently, with the gradual reform of the system, the banks were led into increased securitisation as a means of expanding their turnover. They turned to securing commission from financial facilitation as a source of profit. When a person takes out a loan she is required to secure a certain amount of capital so that there will be some guarantee in the event of the borrower's non-observance of her obligations. But this diminishes her prospects of lending money herself because she is obliged to tie up a certain amount of capital. If someone sells the loan, that is to say issues a security whose holder receives the cash flow from the loan, firstly she is not required to tie up capital, secondly she is able to withhold a proportion of the cash flow *as commission* for issuing the security and so to find a different source of profit, which is directly dependent on the extension of credit that is thereby achieved, that is to say the number of loans that are issued. This nevertheless entails some restrictions. Firstly, in general the expansion of credit contributes to a rise in property values; secondly, the increase in interest rates affects the value of existing securities in the event of conversion into cash or in the event that they are used as collateral for the purpose of obtaining cash. This poses potential dangers of disturbance to the credit system, leading the monetary authorities to judge that they should raise interest rates. Low interest rates, by contrast, facilitate the expansion of credit, under some conditions beyond the limits set by the requirements of capitalist production.

As for the form taken by household finance, it should be borne in mind that competition between individual capitals is conducted through profitable investments exploiting innovations and seeking out unexploited regions or regions that can provide an advantage by comparison with other individual capitals. Banks are not exempt from this rule. Intensified competition in lending to households, insofar as such loans have now come to account for a significant proportion of bank profit, is the basis for issuance of subprimes and other equivalent types of loan, and the basis for effective exploitation of this type of loan within the overall process of securitisation.

(c) Liberalisation has led to excessive expansion of certain banks involved in international transactions which—though for some they represent outmoded practice—are very important *nodal points*, not only from the viewpoint of scale of transactions and obligations but also from that of the links they maintain within the overall context of the international financial system.

(d) Moreover, given the development of "over the counter" (OTC) markets, of various off-shore companies, the development of "Special Purpose Vehicles" (SPVs), of different money markets, bonds, securities, swaps, etc., or in other words the development, in general, of international activities utilising a complex network of financial transactions and money flows that are mostly evading all supervision and/or oversight, the system has become more intricate and complex. At the same time the development of new forms of finance (for example derivatives) has resulted in complex models of pricing and credit risk assessing that depend on parameters for which in all likelihood no data exists. To the extent that information does exist it is likely to be very vulnerable to small changes (to say nothing of its inability to incorporate or measure potential risks and uncertainties created by the complexity of this network of relationships within the capitalist process of production and reproduction). Moreover, in contrast to the ideologies of abolishing the role of the intermediaries what is conspicuous in the current crisis is the emergence of new intermediaries and a network of multiple interlinkages entirely lacking in transparency.

Finally, the emergence and consolidation of the neo-liberal model did not take place from one day to the next. It did not appear as a comprehensive ready-made model but as a process of gradual elaboration taking into account failures, successes and the shifting environment. It did not automatically gain currency in all countries. It appears to have begun to be propagated, though still sometimes in a desultory fashion, following its rise to supremacy in the United States and Britain. For reasons that have to do both with the history of its emergence and with the mode of articulation of international networking, the USA and, to a less extent, Britain have been the centres of the international financial sphere, from which tools, innovations, organisational forms, etc. have been propagated to the rest of the international system. Thus one element at the core of the model is this complex articulation of relations whereby Wall Street (along with other financial centres in the USA) and the City of London have functioned as a centre for dissemination of new regulations and forms of organisation of the financial system.

2. The Relationship between the Financial System and Other Elements Comprising the Core of Neoliberalism

The development of the financial system under neoliberal hegemony is linked to other basic elements comprising the core of the neoliberal model. We will be brief.

(i) One declared objective has been to "deregulate" the labour market as a means of reducing the power of wage-earners to demand wage increases and better terms of employment. This has been pursued both by repressive methods and through monetaristic policies for fighting inflation, and has led to a significant increase in unemployment. It has also been pursued through the weapon of disciplining the behaviour of business and states that is made available through neoliberal money markets. Here it should be noted that monetaristic policies of high interest rates at the beginning of the 1980s, apart from significantly boosting unemployment, also had the result of generating a significant sphere for investment of international capital: higher levels of state indebtedness.

(ii) Moreover—and in one aspect a continuation of (i) — *international trade and outsourcing, that is to say the exposure to international competition for the purpose of devaluing and excluding insufficiently valorised (=non-competitive) capital, are predicated, among other things, on the freedom of movement of capital along with the rest of the neoliberal complex of financial regulation* (non-bank financing, development of differentiated international financial markets). These elements have been mechanisms for schooling labour in the requirements of capitalist restructuring and continuing accumulation. Confining ourselves to the effects that non-bank financing of businesses has had, we detect some significant effects on the mode of operation of these businesses, particularly those that have access to money markets. To name just a very few: *Firstly,* we see *an increase in company debt* in relation to the capital, insofar as the debt increases the profitability of the capital and so sends signals of profitability to the money markets. *Secondly,* for regular continuation of financing *it is demanded* that every enterprise *have high profit indicators*—every suspicion of insufficient valorisation increases the risk of burdensome terms of financing and reduces the companies' competitive potential (e.g. increases the risk of its being taken over). *Thirdly, shares do not comprise the key measure for financing of enterprises* but are raw materials for buyouts and mergers. In other words there is a handling of cash flows and sale and repurchase decisions with shares that increases the share prices (which can play a role in accumulation when what is required is investment that will have a long-term yield). The trade unions, indeed working people in general, experienced these results as loss of bargaining positions. The argument was and is simple: "accept what we propose, otherwise the company will lose its potential for financing". In this case, for example, doubts will be generated as to its profitability and there will be danger of it being bought out, with resultant loss of workplaces, or of the production chain being restructured and a part of the chain transferred to other countries.

(iii) *Privatisation of sectors of state activity and change in the composition of state activities*. Expansion of the space for investment of individual capital is another central element in the neoliberal model. Privatisations are an important factor in bringing about a broadening of the financial sphere. This too has consequences for wage-earners. At a minimum there is a requirement for increased financing of individual needs as distribution "free of charge" is replaced by commodities which have a price (or insofar as the method of costing changes when they pass into the control of private capital). As a result, a basis is created for *an increase in the debt of households* that have access to the banking system; but the potential is also generated for penetration, when required, by banks into new sectors of the market, such as, for example, student loans. Within the same logic as privatisation and greater sanctification of profit is reduction of tax for businesses that contribute to maintenance of high levels of state debt. Reforms to the insurance system have introduced noteworthy pursuers of risk-free profits (insurance companies, mutual capital, hedge funds, etc.) into the company of the banks and so have evidently brought new pressures to bear on wage earners.

(iv) *The securing of consent to the neoliberal model was underwritten by the possibility of access to cheap loans* (in order to finance consumer spending or housing or other expenditure) *and by participation in this global hunt for profits* (among the most conspicuous examples of such participation being the private insurance funds or mutual funds). In this way, the withdrawal of the state from funding universal insurance systems for health, education, social services, etc., will be eased. *Accordingly, the seeking out of potential borrowers, that is to say the incorporation into the credit system of certain groups in the population is not merely the result of the greed of the banks and all types of investor but an injunction that is part of the scheme of neoliberal regulation.* The privately-owned home as a dream that could be made to come true by virtue of neoliberal financial regulation became a declared goal of all representatives of the model. The privately-owned home as an item of property became a means for access to other facilities of the credit system.

From a different viewpoint, the squeeze on wages, a result and objective of the neoliberal model, *also* put a squeeze on consumer expenditure, such that the introduction of appropriate measures to facilitate *consumer credit* became an escape-route for the system, a solution to the problem of managing aggregate demand on the part of the collective capitalist. Today's crisis exposes the difficulties involved in this solution for management of aggregate demand and for organisation of consent to the neoliberal programme. In the place of subprimes one can very readily imagine problems with securities from credit cards and quite likely tomorrow securities from student loans, etc.

3. Banks, Housing Loans and Securitisation

The securitisation of housing loans can be understood as being part of a *production chain*. Let us describe it, employing a minimum of "links".

As raw material we have a form of debt that is accompanied by certain guarantees. The greater the guarantees the greater can be the debt. The bank that issues the loan is required to hold some capital against the loan. Transferring the debt to a third party it can release the capital and start the whole process again. Its profit from the expansion of credit is the commission it receives from ceding credit to a third party. The third party can be another bank or a special purpose company (SPV)[5]. Let us suppose that it is a special purpose company. It gathers together the loans in the form of securities describing a cash flow (instalments) with mortgages as collateral. With the assistance of mathematical financial models (the process of whose "production" comprises another link in the chain, which we propose to leave out of the analysis) it packages them as loans of the same kind from the viewpoint of the credit risk, of delays in payment, of inability to repay and other attendant features, and it issues new securities grouped into different categories in terms of profitability and credit risk (an incomplete description of collaterised debt obligations— CDOs). For someone, e.g. an insurance fund, to be able to purchase securities, she must have a guarantee of the financial "quality" of the securities. *What is thus required is independent evaluation of the securities.* To what extent they can be profitable, that is to say can represent risk-free investments with a "suitable" return, is certified by *credit rating agencies (CRA)*. Certification is important for managers of various entities that are obliged by company regulations only to make risk-free investments (insurance funds, mutual funds) but also for the managers of all companies and other organisations insofar as evaluation of security affects the credit risk they undertake and so the amount of capital they are required to tie up to offset risk in relation to their anticipated profit. Moreover these credit rating agencies are also involved in the process of issuing securities as advisors on the securitisation process on account of the specialised knowledge and the expertise they possess in evaluating credit risk and the "sound" costing of securities.

The next link in this process is the actor who is to purchase the various categories of security. Banks, for the most part, hedge funds, insurance funds. A common practice also is for the category of securities with the highest profitability—that is to say the one that incorporates the greatest risk of suspension of the cash flow and that will be the first to lose from increasing delay in payment of installments by the borrower—to be retained by the issuing bank. It is still, however, not the final link and the ultimate recipient. There are at least two more links that need to be taken into account. Firstly, every person or institution who purchases a security is entitled to take out insurance, so insurance companies are added as a link in the chain, either in the traditional manner or via the CDS (credit default swap) market.[6] Secondly, either the final holder of the security or the SPV is entitled to use the securities as collateral so as to finance her activity in the money market. That is to say, using as collateral securities she has in her possession she is able to take out short-term loans (which she is naturally able to recycle by securing yet other short-term loans). This market is an international market *par excellence* that has developed within the neoliberal model as an alternative to short-term borrowing from banks.

The relationship between banks, SPVs and the money market is the key point around which confidence in the banking system began to collapse. Specifically, when the first signs appeared that securities on housing loans could be facing unpredicted losses, the credit risk for various categories of the relevant securities began to rise. This generated a need for a restriction in the expansion of, and a change in the composition of, the portfolios being held by a number of different finance organisations. The SPV companies, that were dependent for their financing on the ABCP (asset-backed commercial paper) market (that is to say a money market in which short-term loans are issued on the basis of securities), were not able to find disposable resources. This situation was further aggravated by the downgrading of the credit rating agencies examining the creditworthiness of CDO (collateralised debt obligation) securities, which supported the financing of SPVs. The securities in their possession were not easy to sell and in conditions of unpredicted losses any attempt to sell them would reduce their estimated value, thus multiplying the problems for all the financial organisations holding such securities. As result, this inability to secure finance led many SPVs to seek funding through credit lines they had to the "mother" banks as well as to the utilisation of other guarantees that had been agreed upon. All of this happened at a time when the international banks were themselves confronted with a need for larger amounts of capital and limitation of risk. At the same time it was through these actions that there was exposure of a—for the most part unknown—network of informal agreements between the big banks and "affiliated" SPV companies. Insofar as the other players in the financial and credit system did not know what agreements were current between each bank and the SPV companies, there was a more general suspension of confidence, given indeed that the securities being managed by the SPV companies usually involved many times the amount of capital in the "mother" banks.

This situation has led to an increase in interest rates on interbank loans, an increase in demands for collateral, collapse of the CDO securities market and a serious deterioration in the credibility other securities on housing debt, contraction of the possibility of financing through the ABCP market, an increase in risk insurance for all categories of debt and extensive liquidity problems for the big banks—the hub of the international finance system. It has also led many SPV companies to the verge of bankruptcy, forcing the mother banks, in the interest of protecting their own credit-rating, to take back the securities being managed by the SPVs and liquidating them.

There is one point to be remembered here. The relationship between SPVs, i.e. banks, and the money markets shows that the banking and the extra-banking modes of financing are not necessarily antagonistic in their relations with each other. It is just that neoliberal financial arrangements, instead of bringing —as promised—lenders and borrowers into direct contact by abolishing the intermediaries (i.e. the banks), created new kinds of intermediaries, with a more complicated, non-transparent (insofar as the relevant information is personal) and fragile relational structure. For example, the old problem of the relationship between long-term lending and short-term depositing, which banks dealt with internally, has now turned up as an *external*problem between different players on the market: Long-term and illiquid placements on the one hand (the SPVs) and extremely powerful incentives for other players to move freely *en masse* towards whatever, on each occasion, they perceive to be low-risk securities. This is what explains the paradox of having an "excessively bloated" credit system and at the same time minimal liquidity when it is required, given that its functioning is based on securities that are not easily convertible.

The upholding of the liquidity of the system largely by units chasing secure profits which accordingly when they are in doubt reduce the liquidity of the system is not the cause of the crisis but a symptom of the contradictions that activate the neoliberal model. This type of behaviour is a permanent characteristic of the capitalist financing relationship—one must be persuaded that the fiscal plan is worthwhile. Beyond that, the immediate suspension of confidence is employed by the neoliberal regulatory model as a way of disciplining the markets and facilitating profitable business plans and ultimately the composition of the international money markets in which the "cavaliers" of risk-free profit are a constituent element of the model and indeed embody the objective of the model.

4. Interpretations of the Crisis

The reasons for the current crisis can be traced to the contradictory requirements that the neoliberal model for regulating the capitalist economy and its expanded reproduction is called upon to serve. This amounts to saying that it is a systemic crisis in the sense that it has been produced by, and has afflicted, the core of the neoliberal model. We can ascertain this by making a critical survey of the other interpretations of the crisis.

There are interpretations of the crisis that situate it at each of, or all of, the points in the chain of securitisation described above. Before we examine this in detail let us point out that what predominates is a seeking out of causality as synonymous with responsibility: "It is their fault". But the attribution of responsibility to subjects or to extraneous factors is likely to hinder comprehension of the crisis as a crisis engendered by the model of economic regulation itself.

4.1 Subprime Loans as Cause of the Crisis

The commonest approach focuses on the issuing of subprime loans. These are loans that are generally made available to borrowers who do not fulfil some formal requirements for taking out a conventional loan.[7]

These are loans made available to the poorer layers of society and to minorities, which therefore from the viewpoint of the credit system (which bears the greatest credit risk) they also require higher interest rates to counterbalance the risk. But they are also made to borrowers from other income strata who are deeply in debt, as well as those who use this form of borrowing for buying and selling houses. Finally, they represent an opportunity for borrowing for the purpose of rescheduling loans. There are other categories of loans with similar characteristics.

It seems tautological, given that the crisis began with securities on subprime loans, to consider that the issuing of this type of loan is responsible for the emergence of the crisis. Even if we assume that this line or reasoning is correct, it cannot explain why such a crisis did not emerge between 1998 and 2001, when once more there was an increase in delays in paying instalments and so similar problems with the securities issued on the basis of them.

The reasoning is nevertheless fallacious. Not because it is not true, *but because it obscures the factors that operated in such a way as to nurture the crisis and then trigger it.* Why were subprime loans issued? And why were there borrowers who took them out?

The latter question seems to be easier to answer. Firstly, home ownership and the availability of cheap loans to make it possible was a significant factor in the securing consent to the neoliberal programme not only in the USA but also in other developed countries. In the course of development of the conditions for crisis, in 2002 the US president announced the (neo-conservative-oriented) *Homeownership Challenge*, according to which the possession of one's own home was at the heart of the American dream. He then took steps to implement the programme, whose aim was to increase the proportion of homeowners, particularly among minorities (Afro-Americans and Hispanics—those categories of the population among whom four years later one could observe the highest levels of inability to pay off loans and the highest levels of home foreclosures), that is to say to groups mostly excluded from the traditional credit system. To carry out this programme, which "could be implemented only by the state", many organisations responded, offering new types of housing loan so as to increase the options available to borrowers (evidently including the various categories of subprime, which took off spectacularly after 2002). Secondly, through the availability of loans, tax breaks and credit facilities (made possible by the existence of the home as an asset), *the significance of the house itself changes*: It is converted (also)—even when seen as a "roof over one's head"—into a basis for bolstering one's income and as a entry ticket to the facilities provided by the credit system.

Thus, in a context of stagnating real wages and withdrawal of the state from a whole range of social services formerly provided "free of charge", the potential for increasing one's disposable income offered by entry into the credit system (particularly if the mortgage each year increases in value with the increase in land prices) is an important element not only of individual strategies but also of relief from the pressures being exerted by the system. There are other points that could be cited (for example the fact that, depending on the location of the house, one might have access to "more reputable" schools than those in the area of one's current residence), what has been said is nevertheless enough to show that the development of the subprime market was set in motion by profounder elements in the neoliberal model and that today's crisis marks the limits of incorporation of social needs through the neoliberal model. In other words the management of aggregate demand via borrowing and expansion of credit as a means of counteracting constraints on wages is not an effective management mechanism.

As for the first part of the hypothesis, that the issuing of subprimes is simply part of the speculative activity of the bankers who issued them, it is worth stressing that to understand the deeper significance of financial crises it is not useful to make very general references to "speculation" in the sphere of finance. *All business activity is "speculative"*. Every investment of capital aims at securing the highest possible level of profit. The choice of one or the other sphere of economic activity is simply the *means* for achieving the goal. Capital is continually migrating from one sector of business activity to another. It increases or reduces its involvement in the financial sphere. It chooses between production of one commodity or another, its only criterion being to serve the objective of higher profit. References to speculation or profiteering thus offer little to aid comprehension of the specific mechanisms out of which each concrete financial crisis emerges.

Speculation as the reason for the issuing of the subprimes is linked to another more highly elaborated explanation for the appearance of the crisis: the *originate and distribute* (O&D) model for the functioning of banks that has become predominant as banking practice, enabling banks to acquire sections of the market and profitability after the consolidation of the neoliberal model. This is another way of saying the securitisation process.

4.2 *The Securitisation Process or the O&D Model as Cause of the Crisis*

The issuing of subprimes is a product of the capacity for securitisation possessed by the banks that issued them. Given that they simply originated the loan and distributed the risk by selling the securities to others while retaining a commission for that service (O&D: an operational model for banks), they did not have sufficient incentive to examine the quality of the credit underlying the loan they had issued, as they would have had if they had kept the loan on their own balance sheet without being able to transfer it. Because their profitability depended on the volume of securities they issued, they indeed had every incentive to extend credit without too closely examining the risks.

First of all, not all subprime loans are securitized. Securitisation covered 28 per cent in 1995 but this figure from 1998 onwards began to fall, only recovering from 2001 onwards.

In 2001 50 per cent of the value of the subprime loans issued were securitised. This percentage gradually rose to 60 per cent in 2003 and between 75 per cent and 80 per cent from 2004 to 2006. But this is not the important figure when attempting to assess the validity of the above argument.

The relaxation of the regulations and conditions for the issuing of credit, with easy acceptance of guarantees in periods of rapid growth of credit in a context of cyclical economic upturn is a general phenomenon and not something innovatory. In the specific case we are examining, in a context of record low interest rates, low inflation and stable growth in the developed economies, it appears as a natural consequence of the conditions of functioning of credit in a capitalist economy. Note that the relaxing of requirements for issuing of credit, above and beyond questions of incentive, does not involve only the initial issuers of the loans, the banks that securitise the loans, but also involves security holders, as may be seen from the observed general squeeze on the differences between all types of return from interest rates on risk-free securities (a clampdown on credit spreads) *to the pursuit of "normal" profitability of capital.*

One line of explanation for the credit crisis which considers securitisation of loans the *cause* of the crisis, that is to say the transfer of risk outside the portfolio of the lender, because it provides her with incentives to downgrade the quality of loan issuing, has as its *necessary* supplement a second *cause,* which is faulty assessment of the credit risk by the credit rating agencies. Because otherwise one cannot explain why securities were bought which corresponded to low quality loans (unless one evoke the ignorance of "naïve" investors).

Nevertheless, persisting in the logic of "mistakes", that is to say including the "second cause" one is not enabled to explain how many holders of capital (most of them banks with research departments and immediate access to a plethora of data) internationally made a "mistake" in their purchase of securities. It suffices to take into account the common knowledge that higher yields means higher risk insurance and the fact that a certain exchange of written communications between analysts in the international organisations and the central banks has been in public circulation since 2004 at the latest, which made it clear that the methods of price calculation and credit evaluation of CDO departments are "unsound", because they do not take into account a variety of factors.

Here we have to do with the intermingling of practices that are always socially over-determined (and it is on such relations that the elaboration of the specific *mechanisms* is based) such as those of the rating agencies, the lending and securitisation mechanisms, etc. No manager of capital can easily say: "I know that the CDOs are high-risk and not easily sold and for that reason I inform you that this year you will be content with 3 per cent profit. Don't look at others who are earning 9 per cent profit because your money is at risk". In 2001 he would have received the answer: "introduce suitable differentiation into your portfolio, take security measures or risk insurance and throw in some money and we'll see". In 2005 they would have told him he was a fool because others have earned a lot of money by retaining a larger proportion of their portfolio in CDOs. Faced with the demand for guaranteed securities and high profits, in the climate that prevailed after 2001, we can imagine the answer of the bank directors when they find out that they can make money from issuing securities and expanding borrowing, and by falling in with the responses of the remaining parties in the securitisation chain.

But the pursuit of (risk-free) profit on a global scale has never been the privilege of a few. It is the outcome of arrangements (abolition of restrictions) imposed by (and making possible the elaboration of) the neoliberal model and also comprising a prerequisite for it. One consequence of neoliberalism is that a borrower who has lost her house because of a sudden increase in installment payments owing to expiry of the period of grace and insufficiency of her income may simultaneously be a participant in the mutual fund that financed the mortgage-based securities and sought the issuance of the subprimes on account of the greater profitability, as well as being holder of a truncated portion of her pension on account of the fall in value of the securities in which her insurance fund was investing. Her life is thus divided up in the same way as the portfolio whose fate is determined by the good and bad moments for the markets.

Before moving on to the composition of the various factors that have nurtured, and then triggered, the crisis we propose to examine one final point, which is also projected as one of the underlying reasons for it.

4.3 The Bubble in Housing Prices and Low Interest Rates

In the United States a sharp rise in house prices is to be observed between 2000 and 2006, with some areas showing a greater rise than others. For example in Los Angeles and Miami a price rise of more than 160 per cent is to be noted in a period of six years, while in Detroit the corresponding figure is 10 per cent. On the basis of this increase in prices, construction activity starts to grow after 2002, leading to a record high level of supply of apartments in 2006 and probably playing an important role in the falling off in the increase in price rises in 2006, which in turn had an effect on the servicing of debt. Because above and beyond the fact that this period saw the expiry of the period of grace on a great proportion of loan contracts or low-repayment-rate subprimes that had been taken out previously, we have at the same time a hike in interest rates with concomitant difficulties in servicing debts, and simultaneous incapacitation of the chain of loans for buying a house, which you could later reschedule on more favourable terms because its value would have risen. Nevertheless the average increase is considerably smaller, in fact many times smaller, than what was observed in other countries. The reasons for the increase in prices are not traceable only to expansion of credit. They should also be sought out in what was said earlier about the importance of owning one's own home and also in the fact that following the dot.com meltdown the purchase of a house seemed like the next risk-free refuge for investments. Another important factor was of course the record-low interest rates after 2001 and the squeeze on various high-risk premiums.

There is nevertheless a big difference between recognising the importance of the factor of low interest rates and regarding it as the reason for the increase in house prices. Much more so when it takes the form of a proposal that the FED should increase interest rates so as to bring a halt to the bubble in the housing market. For a start, after 2004 when the FED increased interest rates, a doubling in the proportion of subprime loans can be observed (from 335 billion in 2003 to 540 billion in 2004 and 60 billion in 2006). In general after 2004 and the gradual increase in interest rates, the categories of loans being made available included non-conventional variable-interest-rate loans, that is to say the loans through the medium of which the crisis made its appearance. Even worse, the monetaristic-leaning proposal claiming for an increase in interest rates large enough to be capable of curbing the rise in house prices (that is to say quite a significant rise), it amounted indeed to a proposal that the economy should be led into a recession in 2001 so as to avoid the recession of 2008.

5. The Cavaliers of Risk-free Profit and Lives of Precarious Subjection

References to a general characteristic (speculation) or to the imperfections of the mechanism of functioning of the financial system (O&D, faulty assessment, non-correspondence of interests, information imbalance between the parties to a contract, etc.) sheds little light on the two ends of the chain in the crisis process.*The ends of the chain are the most important because they show up the contradictions in the neoliberal model that have nurtured, and then triggered, the crisis.*

The rise in house prices, the issuing of subprimes, securitisation, evaluation of securities, the relationship between SPVs and the money markets... none of these are causes. They are forms of appearance and vehicles for unfolding of the elements and relationships that comprise the neoliberal model, that is to say the particular form of organisation of capitalist social formations after 1980.

Having in the previous sections described the basic elements and the relationships that make up the core of the neoliberal model for arranging the financial system we will confine ourselves here to drawing certain summary conclusions.

(1) The squeeze on salaries and flexibilisation of work relations, that is to say reduction in the bargaining power

of workers against capital, are a success story of neoliberalism but *at the same time* represent one of the conditions for the nurturing and triggering of the crisis. The basic element in the equation is an accumulation of contradictory demands from the financial system. The international order of the "knights of risk-free profit" performs a crucial function for the capitalist mode of production, one that is an inseparable core element of the neoliberal model. But the effects of its action (increasing inequality in income distribution, with reduction in the share accruing to wages, and new types of commodification of human needs) pose problems for management of aggregate demand in the interests of smooth functioning of expanded reproduction and accumulation, as well as problems in organising consent to the model, insofar as restrictions are placed on the capacity for managing the inequalities that are generated through extension of credit to groups that were previously excluded from it. *In other words the conditions for increase in class domination of capital appear simultaneously as conditions undermining that domination.*

(2) The process of the money markets' acquiring "depth", that is to say the process of incorporation into the "International of Capital" of every possible available sum of money that can be deposited in the various separate spheres of the financial system is also a crucial element for the international dimension of the financial system as well as for mobilising the entirety of the capitalist mode of production for the purpose of increasing profitability and accumulation. Thus, for example, it is regarded as a condition for the financial sphere acquiring "depth" that insurance systems be privatised or in any case that flexible criteria for management be developed to enable participation in the international financial system. It represents success for the model that it enriches the markets with numerous players and mobilises every sum of capital that cannot be directly invested in the production process so that it participates in the "club"

of demands on future profit. Without the broader non-bank financing there would be no securing of the mobility of capital and the broader funding potentialities. Without this depth, credit could be destabilised by the failure of a single player. At the same time, however, this "depth" means ever great pressures for risk-free profit, for issuing of securities, in other words for intense competition, so that unexplored markets can be subordinated to the world of credit, with consequent downplaying of risk and massive withdrawal from participation and funding when secure profit is jeopardised.

Let it be noted here that competition between capitals in showing high profit levels, competition which is significantly enlarged and accelerated by the international organisation of finance, as we have seen, means that banks have to extract profits from exploitation of housing loans and from the securities that they issue. This situation coexists with the withdrawal of the state from provision of housing, which now becomes a profit-making activity. This situation in itself means that under the pressure of producing securities and through competition between companies *subprimes will be produced and risks will be downplayed.* The conditions emerge, that is to say, for a crisis to be generated.

(3) In parallel with depth goes the international character, a constitutive element of the model and its success, insofar as the economic world in its entirety is transformed into a "profit chart". The international character together with depth and custodianship of risk management techniques and tools (such as CDS) for ensuring security against risk, ensure greater spread of risk. *A little risk for many and so no great risk for any one party and none for the system as a whole.* But these same elements, depth and the international character, in combination with the demand for security of profit functioned, when the first doubts appeared in relation to the housing credit securities not as factors for

spreading risk but for planetary proliferation of risk. Each individual faces an unknown risk, so let her wait for the storm to blow over so as not to communicate to me also her own risk which is thus the manifestation of a global systemic danger. It is finally worth noting that the "wisdom of the markets", an important element in constructing the core of the neoliberal model, prescribes market evaluation of property (market-to-market value). It is this that has caused the lack of trust between the players because the fall in value of the securities has spoilt the balance-sheets of the institutions maintaining them and protracted the uncertainty. The solution adopted is a familiar one. But the result is that it has become possible for a number of elements not to be factored into the overall assessment.

(4) Before proceeding with characterisation of the crisis, we should note one important point. All these elements of previous crises over the last two decades have functioned through different combinations of factors and to differing extents. Nevertheless, because they did not strike at the heart of the model, it was possible for those seeking to implement it to resort to a dismissive device: the basic idea is sound. It is just a question of applying its principles with greater consistency or at any rate taking measures that don't involve allowing the emerging problems to draw into question the central conception. Today this is no longer possible. The heart of the system has taken a hit and the metaphysical/ideological concessions that continue to legitimate it are treated as such by broader circles.

6. On Characterisation of the Crisis: From Financial Crisis to Crisis of Overaccumulation

The above arguments make it possible for us to characterise the crisis. *It is a crisis that has appeared in the financial sphere and is systemic.* Systemic in the sense that it has been engendered by the elements and the relations that are at the core of the neoliberal model. It is systemic also because it has struck at important nodal points of the system and through them at the terms of operation of the "International of Capital". It is systemic also because it has hit the most powerful organisational centre of the model. The markets and the financial institutions of the United States, which were the key control points for the overall system of organising markets, intervening in them and promoting financial innovations and financial tools. If we take it into account that Britain, the world's second financial centre, has also been affected (and very powerfully), we obtain some picture of how the system has been centrally affected. It is also systemic in that the capacity of the collective capitalist to guarantee the functioning of this arrangement has been incapacitated.

It is not necessary to start again from the beginning, that is to say from housing policy and its financing in the USA. If, at the moment that the crisis has affected an important nodal point of the system measures were taken that approached the problem as a crisis of capital and not just of liquidity, that is to say, in other words, if there had been the Brown plan before the Paulson plan had been formulated (making the latter superfluous) it is quite probable that this crisis would not have assumed the dimensions that it has. There would unavoidably have been a credit squeeze, but quite likely not to the extent, and at the speed, that we have now seen. *In other words the implementation in the collective capitalist's organisation and policies of management of the neoliberal model (e.g. Paulson's policies of defending "self-correction by the markets") up to the "very last minute", played a role in accelerating and spreading the crisis.*

The danger of systemic collapse of the credit system has been minimised by comparison with the situation of several months ago (the days after the collapse of Lehman, in September 2008). Nevertheless, this does not mean that there will not be significant damage to other banks, insurance companies or other private capitals even outside the sphere of the financial system. That is to say, the crisis is still unfolding but it is now taking on the characteristics of a crisis of overaccumulation, which, starting from a ruthless squeeze on the financial sector also drags in other sectors and introduces the economic system as a whole to the operations of liquidation of inadequately utilised capital (obviously at an unequal rate in the different countries and with an intermeshing of the developments in each country both with the developments in other countries and with the financial system).

The interconnectedness of events is thus the reverse of what is often maintained (e.g. Brenner 2008). What is involved is not a continuing crisis of overaccumulation dating from the 1970s, which has fed superfluous capital into the sphere of finance, in this way leading to speculation, the "bubble" and the crisis. The preceding crisis of overaccumulation of capital had already been blunted with the contribution of the neoliberal settlement (in which a decisive nodal point was the functioning of the financial sphere). There had been a return of profits to levels approaching those of the early 70s, production had been restructured, labour made more flexible, wage levels frozen. The share accruing to wages was continually contracting. But the blocking of the sphere of finance and credit funding on which expanded reproduction of capital was based was necessarily translated as "involvement" of this expanded reproduction. It was initially expressed in overproduction of (unsold) goods, given that a credit squeeze implies restrictions on productive and individual consumption (perpetuated by credit). This in turn meant an abrupt fall in profitability and the necessity for cutbacks in production, that is to say lagging dynamism in the means of production, overaccumulation of productive capital, necessity for a new cycle of restructuring.

The latest decision framework, variations on the Brown proposal, for participation of the state in capital or nationalisation of banks and other enterprises, is not an answer for the elements that nurtured and triggered the crisis. There has accordingly been a mobilisation of the international bureaucracy via various institutions suitably inoculated against the "virus" of democracy, and it is now promising to discuss the crisis and take measures to prevent its recurrence.

This is only to be expected. A crisis at the heart of the system puts on the agenda the question of rearrangement and naturally "registration" of the international correlations of power.

Systemic crisis does not necessarily spell destruction for the system. It means exposure of its contradictions. And the representatives of the collective capitalist perceive the situation more or less as follows (on the basis of the current dynamic of unfolding and proliferation of the crisis): that it is a disease that is not going to pass just with a pill but will require some kind of an operation that will enable the *same* organism to continue to function, albeit in a different way, for example without excessive speeding-up. But each attempt at regulation means a redistribution of power and most probably cancellation of functions. However from the new arrangements that are anticipated there will be no interference with the international character of the finance system, securitisation, the deepening of the market, the squeeze on working people. *These are inviolable terms of each new set of arrangements, on the basis of today's strategy of capital. They are strategic options with no fall-back position.* Thus, as perceived by a plethora of organisations and shapers of policy, state intervention must be chronologically limited, must aim exclusively at the generally recognised problem and must leave no trace behind it when the time comes for it to withdraw (particularly traces that would hinder the "free" functioning of markets).

If, then, the core of the neoliberal dogma must remain intact, with mere readjustment of the relations and the pace of the functioning of its constituent elements or the regional machinery (with the overwhelming correlation of power in favour of capital simply taken as a given), the workforce will continue to be treated as the dependent variable, destined to absorb all the shocks, current and future.

Nevertheless, crisis at the heart of the system also entails breaches in the terms of its ideological hegemony. Citizens understand quite simply: if the state intervenes to save the banks why can it not do the same for the insurance funds, for the health system, for...

The traces left behind by the current conjuncture of the crisis do not however require any particular skill to detect. Firstly, discredit is brought to bear on a basic ideology that the state is "bad because it is incompetent" and the markets "good because they are both competent and effective". States are being called upon to act as guarantors of stability, in other words to implement interventionist policies. This is not something easily to be erased from the collective memory. Secondly, the crisis is having adverse effects on the capacity for generating consensus because of the effects it is having on the working population and "underdogs" generally. The limitations of demand management, not through strengthening of wages and the terms of employment but through encouraging excessive household indebtedness, have become evident to all. Both these phenomena strengthen the political forces that seek a different way of managing the capitalist system. From this viewpoint it should not pass unnoticed that P. Krugman (Nobel Prize 2008) in his book, *The Conscience of a Liberal* is in effect calling for state intervention for the creation of trade unions in branches where there is an uninsured workforce, defending the idea of a public and universal health system, demands which make manifest the tension that has been accumulated on account of the polarisation imposed by the class struggle. Thirdly there is a readjustment in the international correlation of power. A reform of the international financial system always harbours an inherent potential that there will be a rewriting of international rules and obligations, thus affording an opportunity for recording the correlations of power that have emerged.

The labour movements cannot comprise part of this new regulation, which is directed against their interests. On the other hand, the crisis for the first time in decades gives them the opportunity to intervene so as to change the correlations of power and impose solutions that secure their own interests in the face of those of capital. One point today is that social insurance is dependent on the profitability of the insurance funds, education on the privately funded "research programmes" and on student loans, work on the international evaluation of the profitability of the enterprise on the world's stock exchanges and financial markets, food on the smooth functioning of the future markets, the operations of the municipalities on mutual funds and international securities markets, the environment on pollution rights, the covering of basic social needs on the level of credit card debt.

In present-day conditions the project of de-commodifying needs, that is to say the defence of social organisation on the basis of freedom in satisfaction of needs and not the repressive calculus of valorisation of capital... is urgent.

(April, 2009)

NOTES

1. In Volume I of *Capital*, it is written: "The monetary crisis defined in the text as a particular phase of every general industrial and commercial crisis, must be clearly distinguished from the special sort of crisis, also called a monetary crisis, which may appear independently of the rest and only affects industry and commerce by its backwash. The pivot of these crises is to be found in money capital, and their immediate sphere of impact is therefore banking, the stock exchange and finance" (Marx 1990: 236).
2. For an interesting analysis of the role of modern financial derivatives, see Bryan and Rafferty (2006).
3. For a Marxian interpretation of the overaccumulation crisis, see Milios et al. (2002).
4. According to Marx, "Overproduction of capital and not of individual commodities—though this overproduction of capital always involves overproduction of commodities—is nothing more than overaccumulation of capital" (Marx 1991: 359). "Periodically too much is produced in the way of means of labour and means of subsistence, too much to function as means for exploiting the workers at a given rate of profit" (Marx 1991: 367).
5. Here we include for purposes of simplicity all the forms of SPV: SIV (structured investment vehicle) and above all banking hedge funds.
6. That is to say the market for contracts by means of which the first party pays the second an insurance premium and the second undertakes to cover losses arising from some more or less formalized events that might have an effect on cash flow or the value of a security in the possession of the first party (for example cessation of servicing of the security's cash flow on the part of the issuer of the security, or premature paying-off of the debt which has the effect of reducing the overall cash flow), in both cases events that have become increasingly prevalent in recent years.

7. One example of such disqualifiers is a bad credit rating, that is to say delays of more than 90 days in paying instalments. Other examples include having an income insufficient to justify the taking out of a loan of such high value, or being employed in a job which does not guarantee a regular flow of payments, or lacking suitable documents that could justify the size of the loan in relation to the client's declared income, etc.

SELECTED BIBLIOGRAPHY

Agarwal, Sumit, 2007. "Comparing the Prime and Subprime Mortgage Markets". *Essays on Issues*, FRB of Chicago, August 2007, No. 241.

Amato, Jeffery D. and H. Furfine Craig, 2003. "Are Credit Ratings Procyclical?", BIS Monetary and Economic Department, Working Papers, No. 129.

Arestis, Philip and Malcolm Sawyer, 2006. *A Handbook of Alternative Monetary Economics*, Edward Elgar Cheltenham, UK• Northampton, MA, USA.

Ashcraft, Adam B. and Til Schuermann, 2008. "Understanding the Securitization of Subprime Mortgage Credit", Federal Reserve Bank of New York, Staff Report No. 318, March 2008.

Berger, Allen N., Anil K. Kashyap, Joseph M. Scalise, Mark Gertler and Benjamin M. Friedman, 1995. "The Transformation of the US Banking Industry: What a Long, Strange Trip It's Been", *Brookings Papers on Economic Activity*, Vol. 1995, No. 2, (1995), pp. 55-218.

Bliss, Robert R. and George G. Kaufman, 2002. "Bank Procyclicality, Credit Crunches, and Asymmetric Monetary Policy Effects: A Unifying Model", Federal Reserve Bank of Chicago, Working Papers WP-2002-18.

Borio, Claudio, 2008, "The Financial Turmoil of 2007?: A Preliminary Assessment and Some Policy Considerations", BIS, Monetary and Economic Department, Working Papers No. 251.

Borio, C., C. Furfine and P. Lowe, 2001. "Procyclicality of the Financial System and Financial Stability: Issues and Policy Options", BIS Papers No. 1, March.

Brenner, R., 2008, "Devastating Crisis Unfolds", IV Online magazine: IV396 - January, http://www.internationalviewpoint.org/spip.php?article1417.

Bryan, D. and M. Rafferty, 2006, *Capitalism with Derivatives. A Political Economy of Financial Derivatives, Capital and Class*, New York: Palgrave Macmillan.

Catarineu-Rabell, Eva, Patricia Jackson and Dimitrios P. Tsomocos, 2003. "Procyclicality and the New Basel Accord—Banks' Choice of Loan Rating System", Bank of England 2003, Working Paper No. 181.

Duménil, Gerard and Dominique Lévy, 2005a. "The Nature and Contradictions of Neo-liberalism".

Duménil, Gerard and Dominique Lévy, 2005b. "Costs and Benefits of Neoliberalism A Class Analysis".

Dymski, Gary A., 2007. "From Financial Exploitation to Global Banking Instability: Two Overlooked Roots of the Subprime Crisis", SOAS Conference, "A Crisis of Financialization?", 2008.05.30.

Feldstein, Martin S., 2007. "Housing, Credit Markets and the Business Cycle", NBER Working Paper 13471.

Fender, Ingo and John Kiff, 2004. "CDO Rating Methodology: Some Thoughts on Model Risk and Its Implications", BIS Working Papers, No. 163.

Goodhart, Charles A.E., 2008. "The Background to the 2007 Financial Crisis". International Economics and Economic Policy Vol. 4, No. 4 pp. 33-346.

Greenlaw, David, Jan Hatzius, Anil K. Kashyap and Hyun Song Shin, 2008. "Leveraged Losses: Lessons from the Mortgage Market Meltdown", US Monetary Policy Forum Conference, New York, February 29, 2008.

Greenspan, Alan and James Kennedy, 2007. "Sources and Uses of Equity Extracted from Homes". Federal Reserve Board, Finance and Economics Discussion Series, Staff Working Papers, 2007-20.

Greenspan, Alan, 2002. *Cyclicality and Banking Regulation*. Conference on Bank Structure and Competition, Federal Reserve Bank of Chicago, Chicago, Illinois.

Jobst, Norbert and Arnaud de Servigny, 2007. *The Handbook of Structured Finance*. McGraw-Hill, New York (chapter 12, 13).

Kregel, Jan, 2007. "The Natural Instability of Financial Markets", *The Levy Economics Institute*, Working Paper No. 523.

Kregel, Jan, 2008a. "Minsky's Cushions of Safety. Systemic Risk and the Crisis in the US Subprime Mortgage Market", The Levy Economics Institute, Public Policy Brief, No.93.

Kregel, Jan, 2008b. "Changes in the US Financial System and the Subprime Crisis", The Levy Economics Institute, Working Paper No. 530.

Krugman, Paul, 2007. *The Conscience of a Liberal*. New York: W.W. Norton & Company, Inc.

Kuttner, Robert, 2007. "The Alarming Parallels between 1929 and 2007". *The American Prospect,* October 2.

Marx, K., 1990. *Capital,* Volume 1, Penguin Classics, London

Marx, K., 1991. *Capital,* Volume 3, Penguin Classics, London.

Marx-Internet 1872. *Capital,* Volume 1.

Marx-Internet 1894. *Capital,* Volume 3.

MEW (Karl Marx/Friedrich Engels - Werke), Band 23. 1968. *Das Kapital,* Bd. I, Berlin: Dietz Verlag.

MEW (Karl Marx/Friedrich Engels - Werke), Band 25. 1983. *Das Kapital,* Bd. III, Berlin: Dietz Verlag.

Milios, J., D. Dimoulis and G. Economakis, 2002. *Karl Marx and the Classics; An Essay on Value, Crises and the Capitalist Mode of Production*. Aldershot, London: Ashgate.

Palley, Thomas I., 2007, "Financialization: What It Is and Why It Matters", The Levy Economics Institute, Working Paper No. 525.

Ruckes, Martin, 2004. "Bank Competition and Credit Standards", *The Review of Financial Studies,* Vol. 17, No. 4, (Winter, 2004), pp. 1073-1102.

Shiller, Robert J., 2007, "Understanding Recent Trends in House Prices and Home Ownership", Kansas City FED, Jackson Hole Symposium 2007.

Wojnilower, Albert M., 1962. "Changes in the Quality of Business Loans of Commercial Banks", *The Journal of Finance,* Vol. 17, No. 4, (December, 1962), pp. 667-668.

Wojnilower, Albert M., M. Friedman Benjamin and Franco Modigliani, 1980. "The Central Role of Credit Crunches in Recent Financial History", *Brookings Papers on Economic Activity,* Vol. 1980, No. 2, pp. 277-339.

Wray, L.R., 2007. "Lessons from the Subprime Meltdown", The Levy Economics Institute, Working Paper No. 522.

Wray, Randall L., 2008. "Financial Markets Meltdown. What Can We Learn from Minsky?", The Levy Economics Institute, Public Policy Brief No. 94.

4

Global Trends, Faultlines and Tectonic Shifts: A Historical Perspective on the 2008-9 Crisis

Bülent Gökay and Darrell Whitman

At the conclusion of his widely popular 1987 study of the global political economy, titled *The Rise and Fall of the Great Powers*, England-born and Oxford-trained Yale historian Paul Kennedy observed, "The task facing American statesmen over the next decades ... is to recognize that broad trends are under way, and that there is a need to 'manage' affairs so that the *relative* erosion of the United States' position takes place slowly and smoothly" (Kennedy, 1989: 534). In chronicling the decline of the US as a global power, Kennedy compared measures of US economic health, such as its levels of industrialisation and growth of real gross national product (GDP), against those of Europe, Russia, and Japan. What he found was a shift in the global political economy over the last 50 years generated by underlying structural changes in the organisation of its financial and trading systems.

Kennedy's arguments about a structural decline in US power are shared by other critical historical thinkers who similarly see global political economy through a historical lens. Andre Gunder Frank (*ReOrient*, 1998), Emmanuel Todd (*After the Empire: The Breakdown of the American Order*, 2002), Giovanni Arrighi (*Adam Smith in Beijing: Lineages of the Twenty-First*

Century, 2007), Niall Ferguson (*The Ascent of Money*, 2008), Peter Gowan ("Crisis in the Heartland", 2009), and Fareed Zakaria (*The Post-American World*, 2008) all use history to argue that US power is declining in parallel to a rise of regional powers, and particularly China. In their view, this decline is not the consequence of "bad behaviour", even if bad behaviour has occurred, but is the function of structural changes that have occurred as the global economy attempts to adapt to changing historical circumstances. Our analysis of the roots of the present crisis similarly finds that historical change has affected the structures of the present system in ways that its original design did not anticipate, and argues along with Frank, Arrighi, Gowan, and Zakaria that these changes are long-term trends that cannot be mitigated by regulatory reform but must be accommodated through structural adaptations that recognise emerging political, economic, and environmental realities that cannot be contained by Euro-American global capitalism.

Immediate Cause of the Present Crisis

As of this writing, economic opinion has converged around a consensus that the immediate cause of the present global crisis was sub-prime mortgage lending in the US that spread through an interconnected global financial system.[1] We argue that this subprime lending, which began in the US in the early 2000s and spread to parts of Europe thereafter, was generated not for the purposes of either providing housing to those previously excluded from home ownership, as many mainstream economists and politicians have argued, but in response to a massive accumulation of capital in the international financial system that required profit-oriented investment.[2] The perception of prosperity was largely fabricated on the basis of a housing boom and highly leveraged real estate speculation. While subprime lending was accompanied by the development of new speculative financial instruments, in operation it functioned as part of a money merry-go-round that was created within global capitalist financial structures to enable the expansion of global capitalism. This expansion involved privatising important elements within the system, such as currency management and banking, in ways that removed them from public scrutiny and regulation.

By closely examining how sub-prime mortgage lending served the global money merry-go-round, we hope to offer insights into the more pernicious features of the global capitalist political economy that have plagued it with recurring economic crises since its creation at Bretton Woods in 1944. Of particular importance has been the role of the US in acting as the economic policeman for this system, and the way that it has encouraged, rather than discouraged, a proliferation of complex investment tools that masked the true nature of underlying capitalist economic activity. In so doing, the US oversaw a structural transformation of international banking that interconnected global financial institutions and exposed them to speculative losses they little understood. This framed the current crisis as the first truly global economic contraction in more than 70 years, making it a direct challenge to continuing US economic and political leadership. As capitalist governments scramble to regain control, they are confronted not only with the failure of US leadership, but also the inadequacies of the Bretton Woods system to accommodate the global shifts and systemic faultlines that now infect global economic and political relationships.

Subprime Mortgages and the Money Merry-go-round

As the term suggests, "subprime" mortgage lending was highly speculative because it targeted potential buyers that otherwise could not qualify for standard home loans. The "subprime" element in these loans was the below-market rate of interest charged during the initial loan period, which would last 3-5 years, depending on the loan terms. However, once the initial period passed, the rate was destined to rise, raising the underlying mortgage payment. Additionally, many, if not most, of these loans were made with little or no down payment, instead of the 5 per cent or 10 per cent usually required in standard home mortgages, down payments were effectively folded back into the original loan, which, when closing costs and fees were added, made the amount of the loan exceed the stated price of the house. The underlying premise of subprime lending was that borrowers would be able to accommodate higher payments in the future, either because their incomes would increase, or because the value of the house itself would continue to rise creating equity for the borrower where none had earlier existed.

The amount of global capital devoted to US subprime lending was staggering, amounting at one point to some $12 trillion in the US alone.[3] Yet, even as sub-prime mortgages carried risks related to their character, these risks were not equally distributed among the borrowers, lenders, and ultimate holders of these mortgages. For example, loan originators, who earned large fees for making but not managing these loans, were exposed only to the risk that the market would collapse, leaving them with few customers. On the other hand, borrowers bore the risk that their income would not keep up with the increase in their mortgage costs, or that the value of their property would decline, leaving them "upside down" on their mortgage, a condition where the value of their mortgage exceeded the value of their house. However, the greatest risk was born by the ultimate holder of the mortgage, because they had no direct knowledge of the actual value of the property, the circumstances of the borrower, or the prospective long-term value of the home. While the low risk, high-profit motive of the loan originators is apparent, and the deferred risk motives of the borrower can be understood, it is still difficult to understand why subprime mortgages became such a major part of the US home loan industry, or why the ultimate holders of these loans would agree to buy them.

On closer inspection, sub-prime mortgages were driven by lending practices that created an illusion of opportunities for risk-free profit. With huge amounts of capital pouring into the US through the purchase of US treasury notes and corporate stocks and bonds, US interest rates, including mortgage interest rates, fell steadily through much of the 2000s. Yet, at the same time opportunities for traditional investments in the US were shrinking as the US increasingly bought more and more of its goods and services from low-wage countries. This created the "problem" of the excess capital requiring new outlets for profitable investment, which was solved by channelling it into real estate at all levels. Sub-prime loans thus became a popular investment because they offered a quick profit to the lending industry, and the appearance of long-term profits to the ultimate managers of the loans, based on the seemingly unstoppable rise in real estate values.

The loan originators in the US were led by Country Wide, which, as its name suggests, was a major national mortgage lender, and Freddie Mac and Fannie Mae, two quasi-public lending agencies that originated home loans on behalf of the US government. These and other smaller lenders were encouraged to enter the subprime market by public officials, who wanted to both appear to generously extend home ownership to the working class and poor and a profitable outlet for money invested in Treasury notes. Seeing the potential for speculative profits, major banks joined the subprime parade by buying up and repackaging subprime loans into investment bundles that mixed them with traditional loans and resold them at a considerable profit to other investors in the US and throughout the world. Along the way, various security ratings services got into the act by offering assurances, for a price, that these bundled loans were AAA rated as low-risk investments. As the money merry-go-round spun faster and faster, generating quick and seemingly risk-free profits to lenders, banks, and the US Treasury, no one seriously questioned how this was possible.

The illusion of risk-free profit was promoted by the way that the global financial system had become enmeshed in a web of privatised, quick-profit schemes generated by capitalist speculators. In the decade between the mid-1990s, when the global economic system was transformed and largely privatised, and the first tremors of crisis in 2007, an alphabet soup of new speculative financial tools emerged. At the time, and under the influence of a powerful capitalist narrative of profit generated by neoliberalism, few asked and even fewer understood how these tools worked, but several have now been demystified and exposed as reckless, if not criminal, covers for looting the system. One of the most popular tools was a financial "derivative", such as the bundling and reselling of sub-prime loans, which simply referred to several ways of disguising the nature of an investment and its risks from potential investors. Citibank, Morgan Stanley, and Lehman Brothers were major sources of these derivatives, which earned them huge profits during the 2000s. A second and particularly onerous tool was the "credit default swap" CDS, which acted as form of insurance to cover the risk that an investment might go sour. American International Group (AIG), which was a relatively small insurance company in the 1990s, gorged itself on CDSs during the 2000s to become among the largest insurers in the global market. But unlike a prudent insurer, AIG paid out the fees it earned for issuing a CDS to its own corporate officers and shareholders, keeping only a minimum of capital in reserve. As investigators subsequently discovered, driven by insane profits none of these capitalist corporations did much to determine the actual risks involved in derivative or CDS investments, leaving the entire structure of global finance exposed.

For their part, subprime borrowers, who were generally members of the working class that had long been excluded from home ownership, either accepted subprime mortgages because they were their own choice, or were pushed into it by the lenders who saw them only as profit opportunities. Before the credit crunch, mortgage providers were giving out home loans worth 125 per cent of the value of the property, stretching homeowners way beyond their means. Few of them, however, had any real knowledge of how subprime mortgage lending worked, or about the longer-term risks that they accepted along with their subprime loans. Rather, lenders commonly enticed their applications by assuring them that the risks were small and that they would be able to manage the loan in the future because housing prices would continue to rise, allowing them to either sell for a profit or take out a second mortgage to cover the difference. Once the loan approved, these lenders disappeared, leaving the borrowers to grapple with the consequences as the lenders escaped with their fees as the loans themselves were sold and then resold to other investors.

How Banks Failed

The money merry-go-round of subprime lending could not have developed without the changes in the global financial system that allowed for the accumulation of the vast amounts of capital that it required. These changes, generally understood as neoliberal reforms, included both the promotion of new privatised financial investment tools, and the deregulation of banking, which spread through the US-controlled Bretton Woods economic system through its interlinking of global financial institutions. This allowed high-risk subprime mortgages to insinuate themselves into the fabric of ongoing financial activities without a test of their underlying value. As a consequence, second-, third-, fourth-, and fifth-tier investors, many of them international banks, were never required to account for the value of the subprime mortgages that they held, until the system began to unravel in 2007.

Looking at the current crisis as interlinked problems with the valuation of bank assets, it is easier to see how the collapse of sub-prime lending acted to constrict the free flow of money necessary to keep the global capitalist system working. The first chapter in this story came when world stock markets peaked and began a sympathetic decline in October 2007, signalling that a global rather than national economic crisis was unfolding. The role of banking in the crisis then became apparent when news of a sharp drop in the profits of Citigroup led to a sharp fall on the New York Stock Exchange in January 2008, which then spread to global markets on January 21 as other US and European banks disclosed they also had suffered massive losses in 2007. Thereafter, several key financial dominos in the global system began to fall, beginning with the venerable Wall Street investment bank Bear Sterns, which was rescued by the US Federal Reserve in a controversial move in March 2008 that merged it with the Bank of America as it was nearing bankruptcy.[4] The crisis was held in relative suspension for the next several months as capitalist speculators debated how US government actions might rescue the global economy through various stimulus schemes that would inject hundreds of billions of dollars into the US national economy, and through various schemes that would rescue the US banking system. The debate ended, however, in September 2008 when Lehman Brothers, a 158-year-old international investment bank and one of the largest financial institutions in the US, was forced into bankruptcy.

The failure of Lehman Brothers was immediately caused by the reluctance of the US government to step in with yet another bank rescue, which was attributed to a split within capitalist policymakers between those that favoured purely "free-market" economics that would allow any institution to fail in a competitive marketplace, and liberal capitalists who argued that Lehman Brothers was "too large to fail" because its failure would trigger a "credit crunch", or inability of banks to provide loans except to their very best customers, as banks withdrew from lending in the face of uncertainty about loan risks. The decision to let Lehman Brothers fail first demonstrated that the risks of a credit crunch were very real, but also revealed how governments played a key role in managing capital markets. The relationship between banks and the government economic management had been first raised by commentators with the rescue of Bear Sterns, who observed that its rescue was required "to prevent key financial players from going under",[5] but without noting just who qualified as a "key" financial player. Because the capitalist markets reacted favourably at the time, the rescue of Bear Sterns became a further argument in favour of rescuing Merrill Lynch, Goldman Sachs, and Morgan Stanley, three other giant investment groups, after Lehman Brothers failed. Thus, gripped by fear of a total financial meltdown the US government began to pour hundreds of millions of dollars directly into major US banks, predicated on the ability of this rescue, deemed the "Toxic Asset Relief Programme" (TARP), to relieve the speculative pressures that were enveloping the US banking system. However, this too failed to stem the crisis and other and even larger and more visible interventions by the US and other capitalist governments followed during the Fall of 2008 and Winter of 2009—which together were the largest synchronised government interventions in markets since the 1930s.

Even as the US and European governments coordinated action in November 2008, the crisis intensified in the US and Europe, and spread to other national banks and economies, with a particularly vicious impact on those, such as Iceland, that had been most active in the global financial system. This radically changed forecasts about the global economy, with the International Monetary Fund (IMF) first revising its projections for real global 2008-9 GDP growth downward in November 2008 to 3.7 per cent in 2008 and 2.2 per cent in 2009, against its earlier projections of 3.9 per cent in 2008 and 3.0 per cent in 2009.[6] It also saw that the distribution of growth would be uneven, with advanced economies actually contracting by 0.25 per cent in 2009, which would be its first annual contraction for those countries since World War II, and 2009 GDP growth in emerging economies receding to 5.1 per cent, instead of the 6.1 per cent earlier forecast. Most notably, the IMF predicted the US economy would shrink in 2009 by 0.7 per cent and the UK would suffer the greatest decline among Western European countries by contracting 1.3 per cent. Taken as a whole, these projections meant that emerging economies would provide all real global GDP growth in 2009 and bear the burden of rescuing global economic performance after 2010.[7]

The revisions made by the IMF in November quickly proved inadequate, and it was forced to update them again on January 28, 2009, projecting even slower growth, with the world economy assuming its slowest pace since World War II. In this case, overall growth was expected to be only 0.5 per cent in 2009, with economic activity contracting in the US by 1.5 per cent, in the Eurozone by 2 per cent, and in Japan by an even greater 2.5 per cent. This revision also projected that growth in the developing economies of China and India would decrease to 5.75 per cent and 5 per cent respectively, thus limiting their ability to act as major engines for the world economy.[8] This led IMF chief economist Oliver Blanchard to admit, "We now expect the global economy to come to a virtual halt." Then, in March 2009 the IMF further warned that the world economy would likely contract this year in a "Great Recession" that would be "the worst performance in most of our lifetimes".[9]

The IMF was not alone in its gloomy assessment as the World Bank reported in December 2008 in *Global Economic Prospects 2009* that world trade would contract in 2009 for the first time since 1982, with the decline driven primarily by a sharp drop in demand as the global financial crisis imposed a rare simultaneous recession in high-income countries and a slowdown across the emerging economies.[10] At the national level, the US Federal Open Market Committee (FOMC) similarly revised its earlier economic projections on February 18, 2009, predicting that 2009 economic growth would slow further, while inflation and unemployment would increase.[11] These revisions were understandably hostage to the crisis itself and further revisions were likely to follow that would drive down expectations even further.[12]

As dark as these dark forecasts were, they represented a conservative view by mainstream capitalist economists who tried to put the best face on events. Thus, these reports minimised or ignored how this and earlier crises imposed long-term structural damage on the global economy, choosing rather to blandly predict an economic "recovery" in 2010, based on past experience rather than on the crisis's peculiar global and financial characteristics. For example, in its 2009 forecast the IMF forecast a 2010 recovery with the caveat that the economic contraction would be more prolonged in certain countries, including the US and the UK.[13] Yet, with past experience as a guide these official forecasts look increasingly weak as new measurements of economic activity reveal a much deeper annual decline in the US fourth quarter GDP, far beyond the 3.8 per cent earlier estimated, with private US investment falling in that quarter at a 21 per cent annual rate and the Japanese economy contracting at a 12 per cent annual rate.[14] Thus, prudence argues that official estimates be seen more as self-interested "guesstimates" than as fact, with a parade of downward revisions into the future.

All these separate facets of the current crisis came together in the banking system because each of them lowered the underlying value of bank assets, which limited the ability of banks to provide credit. With an integrated global economy functioning through an interconnected financial system, whatever happens within the system, whether at the centre or periphery, becomes a factor in determining the value of assets held by banks. This creates a circular process, where a crisis in any part of the global economic system translates into financial factors that feed into global finance creating a crisis in proportion to the weight of the initial crisis that initiated the cycle. Thus, because the US dominates the global economy and leads its financial sector, its sub-prime mortgage lending and crisis of confidence in bank assets has become the defining factor in generating a global financial and now economic crisis. As political economists understand, this is what makes economics political and not just a collection of calculations.

It also is the case that the effects of the global crisis will not be evenly shared among developed or developing economies, and what happens within the countries of the EU will differ, and in some cases significantly, from what happens in the US or Japan. This is borne out by the way the new central and eastern European members of the EU and the poorer economies in the global system are experiencing the crisis with far more limited resources, tools and prospects,[15] and is chronicled in the plight of developing economies that have already been forced to seek emergency funding from the IMF and World Bank, or face the dark near-term prospect of not meeting their basic needs.[16]

(June, 2009)

NOTES

1. Sub-prime mortgages carry a higher risk to the lender (and therefore tend to be at higher interest rates) because they are offered to people who have had financial problems or who have low or unpredictable incomes.
2. In "Global Imbalances and the Financial Crisis" (Council on Foreign Relations, *Special Report No. 44*, March 2009), Steven Dunaway characterized this development as "imbalances between savings and investment in major countries", which he attributes to flaws in the international financial system that allowed governments, as well as private investors, to evade the consequences of their economic choices.

3. John Gittelsohn, "Ex-subprime Exec Works Flip Side of the Market", *The Orange County Register,* March 16, 2009.
4. The US Federal Reserve is a quasi-public central banking system managed by a board whose members are appointed by the US President and confirmed by the US Congress, but who act independently of both political institutions in setting US monetary policy. This independence in the past has led to conflicts between the political interests of the US government and the economic interests of private US banks when the Fed acts to protect financial capitalist at the expense of the interests of industrial capitalist.
5. Neil Irwin and David Cho, "Fed Takes Broad Action to Avert Financial Crisis", *Washington Post,* March 17, 2008.
6. Gross domestic product is a measure of economic activity in a country that aggregates all the services and goods produced in a year. There are three main ways of calculating GDP by measuring national output, income and expenditure.
7. "World Economic Outlook Update: Rapidly Weakening Prospects Call for New Policy Stimulus", IMF, November 6, 2008.
8. "World Economic Outlook", IMF, January 28, 2009.
9. "Global Economy to Contract in 'Great Recession,' IMF Warns", *Reuters,* March 10, 2009.
10. "Prospects for the Global Economy", *Global Economic Prospect 2009,* World Bank, December 9, 2008.
11. "US FED: Fed Worsens Projections For 2009 GDP, Inflation, Unemployment", *Forbes.com,* February 18, 2009.
12. It should be understood that official projections rely on economic data generated by governments, and that in the US the process of producing this data has become highly politicized with the process of data collection and reporting increasingly tilted toward underreporting politically sensitive data.
13. Shobhana Chandra and Alex Tanzi, "US Economy May Shrink 1.5% in 2009 as Recession Stymies Fed", *Bloomberg.com,* January 13, 2009.
14. Connor Dougherty and Kelly Evans, "Economy in Worst Fall Since '82", *Wall Street Journal.com,* February 28, 2009.
15. See, e.g., "How to Prevent a Financial Crisis in Hungary and Avoid a Domino Effect", January 2009.
16. "Global Short-term Growth Revised Downwards as Economic Prospects Deteriorate", *Euromonitor International,* November 27, 2008.

5

Is 'It' Over? A Look at the Current Economic Crisis

Rohit

Hyman Minsky, an American Economist, had written a book titled *Can It Happen Again* with 'it' standing for the Great Depression of the 1930s, the biggest and the longest economic crisis in the history of capitalism. The answer to this question today seems to be in the affirmative if one takes a deeper look at the events that have unfolded in the financial markets in the United States and the other advanced countries over more than two years. The extent of this crisis, in particular in the US, has led the economic pundits to describe the present financial crisis as something similar to what happened during the 1930s. Despite all the signs of recovery, we believe it is too early and erroneous to assume that the crisis is over and that the government should withdraw the stimulus package.

Theoretical Overview

To place the issues in perspective, it is important to reflect upon the economic ideas that developed regarding growth and crisis under capitalism since the 1930s. In the aftermath of the Great Depression, John Maynard Keynes, a British economist and Michal Kalecki, a Polish economist, had written extensively on its causes as well as its remedies. Though their political orientation was very different (Kalecki was a Marxist while Keynes was not), both argued that it was the absence of direct intervention of the government in the working of the economy and financial markets that led to the Great Depression. The remedy that Keynes suggested was a categorical rebuttal of the principles of *laissez faire* since he asked not only for a regulation of the financial markets but for a direct government intervention to boost the demand in the economy through positive fiscal stimulus. The fiscal management[1] on the lines of the Keynes-Kalecki produced the Golden Age of capitalism in the 1950s and the 1960s in the advanced capitalist countries which saw the longest period of booms in these countries and distribution of income moving partially in favour of the working class.

In the early 1970s, this model broke down and there was a resurrection of the old ideology of free market and finance. It is interesting to note the complete reversal in economic ideas as well as policies despite having learnt the lesson the hard way in the 1930s. It seems almost as if the Keynes-Kalecki were erased from history. But the real answer to this reversal comes out quite clearly in Kalecki's writings. Kalecki, unlike Keynes, looked at capitalism as fundamentally an antagonistic system. Kalecki (1943) argued that even though it is *theoretically* possible to attain high levels of employment and growth through government spending, it cannot go on in the long run. He argued that a prolonged period of low unemployment increases the bargaining power of the workers due to the declining reserve army of labour. Why this would lead to problems in maintaining such a growth process is for the following reason,

> [T]o maintain the high level of employment. . . . in the subsequent boom, a strong opposition of 'business leaders' is likely to be encountered. . . lasting full employment is not at all to their liking. The workers would 'get out of hand' and the 'captains of industry' would be anxious 'to teach them a lesson'.
>
> [U]nder a regime of permanent full employment, 'the sack' would cease to play its role as a disciplinary measure. The social position of the boss would be undermined and the self assurance and class consciousness of the working class would grow. Strikes for wage increases and improvements in conditions of work would create political tension. . . 'discipline in the factories' and 'political stability' are more appreciated by business leaders than profits.

> Their class interest tells them that lasting full employment is unsound from their point of view and that unemployment is an integral part of the normal capitalist system.

So, the reserve army of labour is a *necessity* under capitalism to maintain the correlation of class forces in favour of the capitalists and rentiers. Accordingly, one could argue that the so-called golden age of capitalism was more of an *aberration* than a rule under capitalism. Seen in light of this argument, the present crisis, its severity notwithstanding, is actually not an *exception* but a rule under capitalism. We would like to argue, therefore, that this crisis should not be seen *only* in the light of the failure of the financial system for it could actually be just a signal of deeper malaise in the real economy. This distinction between real and financial crisis is very important because a sizeable majority in the academia and policy circles are arguing that if only the financial markets could be controlled, such crises would not take place. In other words, capitalism otherwise is a stable system provided the financial markets are regulated. Our argument is that crises of this nature can and do take place under capitalism independent of whether the latter were regulated or not. Unregulated financial markets *add* to the severity of the crisis.

Let us concentrate on the sources of malaise in the real economy. Unfettered development of capitalism leads to greater monopolisation by big business. Greater monopolisation of the market ensures a downward rigidity in prices and, therefore, a guaranteed profit margin. On the other hand, there are continuous efforts to improve labour productivity so as to keep the wage costs low. Downward rigidity in prices and continuous increase in labour productivity results in a tendency towards increasing profit share in the total output. While this strategy sounds good for an individual capitalist, it has seeds of its own destruction inbuilt into it.

A higher profit share for the economy *as a whole* leads to a decline in the domestic market. This is so because workers consume a higher proportion of their income than the capitalists and any shift of total income away from workers would *ipso facto* lead to a decline in overall consumption demand in the economy[2]. Since private investment is the main source of growth under capitalism, such a signal of declining consumption in the market exerts a downward pressure on the rate of growth. This is the typical realisation crisis in Marxian terminology. This is an imminent tendency under capitalism because there is no spontaneous mechanism of coordination of investment decisions of the capitalists to avert such a crisis. The reasons for why the system is not under *perpetual* crisis but faces it only intermittently have to be found elsewhere but this tendency exists all the time. The factors which counter this tendency could be state intervention, export-led growth, capitalists' consumption led growth. Each of these factors has different consequences on the trajectory of the growth process, some of which we would focus on later in this article.

Just as the pre-Golden Age, the current period is also not fundamentally different. Inequalities in income and wealth have been rising dramatically since the late 1970s across the world, except for the possible exception of France and Japan, creating conditions for realisation crisis. The genesis of the present crisis lies precisely in the factors which had kept the growth going even when such a tendency existed. Therefore, to understand the present crisis, we need to analyse the economic booms that the US has witnessed in the present decade and the previous one.

Growing Inequality

There has been a dramatic increase in inequality in the US since the early 1980s. What the US is witnessing today in terms of inequality has only one parallel in its history, i.e. the period during the Great Depression (see Fig 1). The inequality is such that the top 10 per cent of the population earns close to 40 per cent of the total income. The inequality has increased in the US since the early 1980s primarily because of two reasons. On the one hand, the income of the poor has got squeezed due to a decline in the legal minimum wages, unionisation rates and increased globalisation, all of which have decreased their bargaining strength. On the other hand, the payrolls of the top executives, especially CEOs, has increased manifold in the absence of either the wage controls of World War II or the social norms of the Golden Age period which restricted the growth of high-end wages.

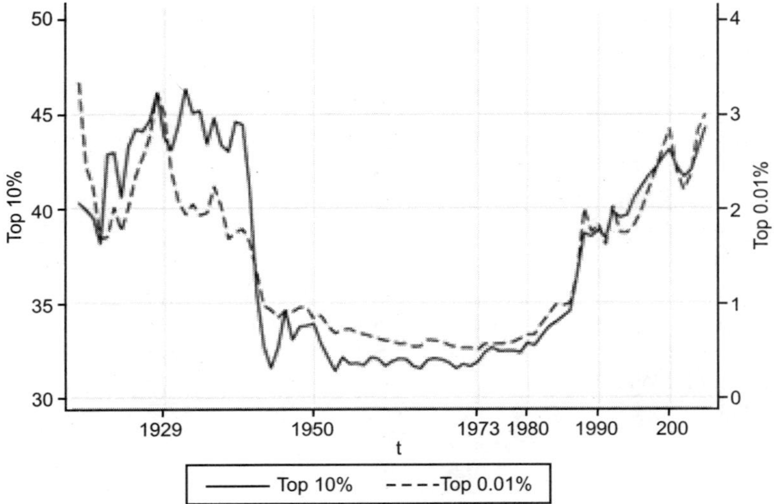

Soure: Piketty and Saez (2003), in updated version

Fig. 1. *Share of Top 10% and 0.01% in the Total Income in the US, 1917-2005*

The increase in equality is not restricted to income alone but there is a growth in wealth inequality too as shown in Table 1. While the top 1 per cent of the population owned 33.8 per cent of the total wealth of the economy, the bottom 40 per cent of the population owned less than 1 per cent of the total wealth in 1983. The wealth inequality increased by 1995 to such an extent that the top 1 per cent owned close to 40 per cent of the wealth while the bottom 40 per cent owned a mere 0.2 per cent.

A major part of the increase in the wealth of the rich during this period has been through the increase in the stock market prices of the financial assets that they own. Since the ownership of stock market assets itself is extremely skewed in favour of the rich, an increase in the prices of the shares has an asymmetric effect in favour of the wealth of the rich.

Table 1. The Extent and Change in Wealth Inequality

Size Distribution	*Top 1%*	*Top 20%*	*2nd 20%*	*3rd 20%*	*Bottom 40%*
Total Wealth					
1983	33.8%	81.3	12.6	5.2	0.9
1995	38.5	83.9	11.4	4.5	0.2
Financial Wealth					
1983	42.9	91.3	7.9	1.7	–0.9
1995	47.2	93.0	6.9	1.4	–1.3
Mean Wealth (in 000, '95 Dollars)					
Total Wealth					
1983	6,708	808.3	124.9	52.9	4.4
1995	7,875	858.1	116.8	45.9	0.9
% change	17.4	6.2	–6.5	–11.5	–79.6
Financial Wealth					
1983	6,187	658.3	57	12.3	–6.3
1995	7,400	730.0	54	11.3	–10.6
% change	19.6	10.9	–5.3	–7.8	–68.3

Source: Wolff (1998)

The Boom of the 1990s

From the point of view of classical political economy, such a growth in inequality should have led to stagnation in the economy instead of a boom as witnessed both in the late 90s and the present decade (prior to the current crisis). If that is the case, then why did the growth of inequality lead to an *increase* in the growth rate in the US in the late 90s and 2000s?

As mentioned above, at least theoretically, there could be three ways which can help avert this tendency towards stagnation into becoming a reality. First, the government could prop up the domestic demand through fiscal management. But this route was practically unavailable given the right-wing dominance in the policy circles which wanted to restrict the role of the government in the real economy[3].

Second, the stress of growth could divert in favour of export-oriented strategy. Again to do that, one needs to be internationally competitive both in terms of technology as well as wage costs, neither of which was in favour of the US. The US had been left far behind in terms of technology by its European counterparts, especially Germany and Japan in Asia.

Third, consumption of the rich could more than compensate for the declining share of workers' consumption through injection of consumption demand independent of the current stream of income, say through the wealth effect coming from the asset price markets. Furthermore, new methods of enticing even the workers to consume through credit financing could also act as a counter to this tendency. It is the third route which the US has adopted in the last two booms which we focus upon in the rest of the paper.

The way this third route worked is the following. Stock or housing market booms led to a growth in the 'notional' wealth of the rich which had a positive effect on the consumption of the rich, a phenomenon called the 'wealth effect'. Increase in consumption due to wealth effect was an external injection of demand into the economy independent of the redistribution of income between the rich and the poor. Though the exact effect of an increase in wealth on consumption in the US has been estimated to be not more than 3 cents per dollar, i.e. out of every dollar increase in wealth only 3 cents are spent on consumption, the sheer magnitude of the wealth increase due to the stock market boom of the late 1990s was such that it had a huge impact on the overall consumption. The argument can be better understood if we look at the exact increase in the wealth of households which increased by 50 per cent within a span of five years between 1995 and 2000. The increase in consumption as a proportion of GDP was close to 1.5 per cent during these years. Therefore, this increase in wealth alone explains the increase in consumption of the household during this period.

A more interesting question, however, is not why the consumption increased but *how* was this consumption *financed*? To understand that, we need to explain how the increase in the wealth was 'notional'? It was purely 'notional' to the extent that its value had increased due to higher valuation in the stock market so that the increased wealth could not be realised from the stock market by all the stock holders at the same time. Any attempt to 'realise' the increased value of the wealth in the stock market by selling the stocks at their higher prices by *all* the investors at the same time would have meant a collapse in the stock market itself. Thus, the increase in wealth was merely notional. That being the case, any increase in expenditure on consumption based on this increase in wealth had to be financed by taking more debt based on the increased collateral in the form of enhanced value of wealth. It is here that the debt spiral began in the US. Therefore, the debt spiral became a *necessity* for the economy to compensate for the imbalances in the real economy.

During the 1990s, the household debt stood at 95.6 per cent of the total disposable income of that sector (see Table 2). In other words, the household debt was almost equivalent to the total income of the sector as a whole in the 1990s. Such high levels of debt-income ratio were ominous signs for the US but the Federal Reserve did not pay attention to the dangerous growth in the debt-income ratios, instead they were busy propagating the argument that the US economy had entered a new phase of 'new economy' where business cycles were a thing of past.

Such sleight of hand by the mainstream economics, however, had to face the reality when the economy witnessed

Table 2. Financial Indicators for the US Economy: 1960–2008.1

(in %)	1960–69	1970–79	1980–90	1991–'00	2000–'08
S&P 500 real average annual growth rate	4.6	-5.9	8.3	14.5	2.28
S&P 500 real growth minus GDP real growth	0.2	-9.2	5.4	11.3	–0.4
Total HH Debt/ Disp Pers Income	67.3	67.6	77.2	95.6	130.08
Total HH Debt/ Financial assets	17.5	20.5	23.1	22.8	30.32
HH bank deposits+govt. sec/ Financial assets	23	25.9	26.7	18.8	15.96

Source: First Four Columns from p. 228, Pollin (2005) and last column author's calculation from the Flow of Funds Accounts of the Fed

the Dotcom bubble go burst in 2001. The business cycle was back as indeed it is a part of the working of any normal capitalist economy, contrary to the claims of the new economy enthusiasts. A decline in the stock market meant a decline in the wealth of the households too and the increased wealth effect was bound to reverse but the debt taken against the increased wealth earlier remained nonetheless.

The Mortgage Boom of the 2000s and the Seeds of Destruction

In the event of the stock market meltdown in 2000, the financial speculators moved away from the stock market to some other avenues where they could make a quick buck and the best opportunity they found was in the housing market. Such a huge diversion of funds from the Dotcom bubble to the housing market had a positive effect on the housing prices just as it had on the stock prices of the IT sector during the late 90s.

An increase in the housing prices made housing into a profitable venture for the household sector because in common perception it was thought to be a safer asset that the stocks, little was it known that it was merely a shifting of one bubble to another. As happens in the stock market, the increase in buyers of houses led to a further increase in prices of housing much beyond its cost of manufacture.

The policy of the government in the post-2001 phase was multi-pronged to provide a boost to the household demand (either in consumer durables or expenditure on housing) which had been responsible for the growth in the 1990s. First, there was a major tax cut by George W. Bush announced on June 7, 2001. Bush, in his remarks in Tax Cut Bill Signing Ceremony, argued that the magnitude of the tax cut that his administration was announcing can only be comparable to the Reagan Tax cut of the 80s or the Kennedy Tax cut of the 60s. This tax cut had a definite impact on increasing the consumption of the rich because they were the biggest beneficiary of the Bush Tax Cut. That is why despite the meltdown in the stock market which had driven the consumption during the 90s, consumption of the household did not decline as would be expected based on the wealth effect (after increasing for over two decades, the consumption share after 2001 remained stagnant instead of declining despite the meltdown in the stock market). The declining wealth effect was compensated to an extent by the easing tax effect during this period.

Second, after the stock market crash of 2000, which had its repercussions well into 2002, the Fed was looking for other ways of stimulating consumption demand because that had been the bedrock of growth in the late 90s. In the absence of another equity price bubble, the housing market provided an opportunity of such an alternative. The prices in the real estate market had been increasing since the mid–90s but it was still a sideshow to the stock market boom of the 90s. It was only in the early years of the present decade that they started picking up. The reason for this housing market run was quite obvious. The stock market crash led the investors to look for alternative measures of keeping their money and real estate seemed a good opportunity because its demand was going high so there was always a potential of making capital gains (p. 92, Pollin (2005)). A Special Report (2005) of *The Economist* had the following to say about the magnitude of the housing market boom in the US or perhaps the entire developed world,

> [T]he total value of residential property in developed economies rose by more than $30 trillion over the past five years, to over $70 trillion, an increase equivalent to 100% of those countries' combined GDPs. Not only does this dwarf any previous house-price boom, it is larger than the global stock market bubble in the late 1990s (an increase over five years of 80% of GDP) or America's stock market bubble in the late 1920s (55% of GDP). In other words, it looks like *the biggest bubble in history*. [Emphasis added]

The extent of speculation in the housing market can be measured by the ratio of the housing prices to the rental applicable to the houses. This is similar to the Price-equity (P/E) ratio of stocks because the income that can be imputed from owning a house comes from the rental that it would fetch in future. Let us see what happened to this ratio. Weller (2006) presents the data comparing the Housing Price Index to Rental and the CPI (see Fig. 2).

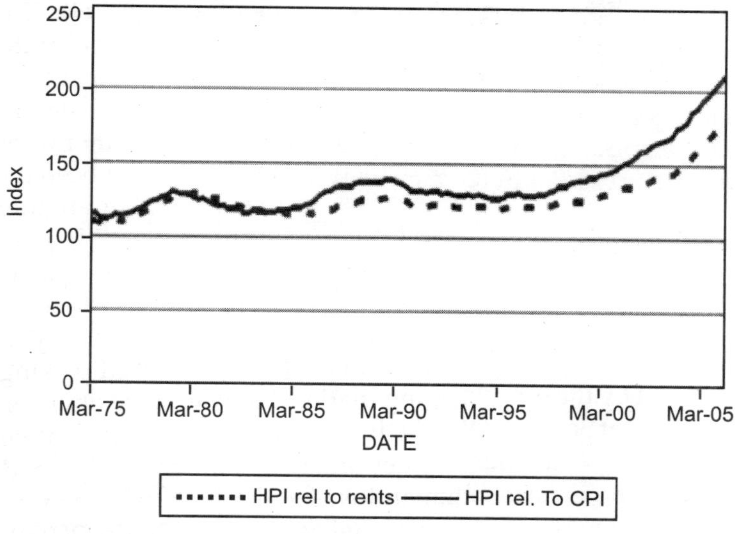

Soure: P. 6, Weller (2006)

Fig. 2. *The Ratio of Housing Price Index to Rentals and the Consumer Price Index in the US*

While the ratio of HPI to rentals remained stable for more than two decades since 1975 (as shown by the dashed line in Fig. 2), there was a sharp increase in it since 2000. This is further corroborated by the fact that in 2004, 23 per cent of the homes bought were purely for investment purposes while 13 per cent were bought as second homes. 'Investors [were] prepared to buy houses they [would] rent out at a loss, just because they [thought] prices will keep rising–the very definition of a financial bubble.' (Report (2005)). In Miami, nearly half of the original buyers resold their apartments in an attempt to make capital gains.

In such a situation of high speculation, the Fed pushed aggressively for an easy monetary policy which meant a drastic decline in the federal funds rate (short term interest rate set by the Fed) even below the rate of inflation resulting in negative real funds rate. The real federal funds rate remained negative from mid-2002 to early 2006 which meant a real heavy dose of easy money for more than three years. This kind of monetary policy has not been seen in the recent past in the US. The household sector responded very positively to this easy credit policy because the mortgage rates also declined. They increased their expenditure on housing which further increased its prices and the spiral started building up. This was the other bubble building up as Pollin (2005) writes (p. 92),

> As the upward price momentum continued through the middle of 2002, the *Wall Street Journal*, among other observers, began warning of the dangers of a housing "market bubble" in which "stretched buyers push mortgages to the limit."

The "limits" to which the buyers were "pushed" can be estimated by the growth in the Financial Obligation Ratio (FOR) and the Debt Service Ratio (DSR) of the household sector during this period. Debt Service Ratio (DSR) is the ratio of debt payments on outstanding mortgages and consumer debt to the disposable income of the household sector. We also present data of a more inclusive concept of the debt obligation that the household sector holds. This measure is called the Financial Obligation Ratio (FOR) which, apart from the repayment of interest charges on outstanding mortgage and consumer debt, includes the automobile lease payments, rental payments on tenant-occupied property, homeowners' insurance, and property tax payments.

Some important conclusions can be drawn about the financial condition of the household sector based on these two ratios. In panel (a) of Fig. 3, it clearly shows that both DSR and FOR have been rising since the early to mid–1990s. If we differentiate between the debt payments on account of home mortgages and consumer durables, we get panel (b), which tells us another interesting story behind this debt growth. As expected, for the 1990s, which is characterised by stock market boom, it is the consumer durables debt payments that play a central role in driving the FOR up, whereas the home mortgage debt payments were declining for that decade. After 2000, however, when the real estate boom replaced the stock market boom, it is the home mortgage payments which determine the

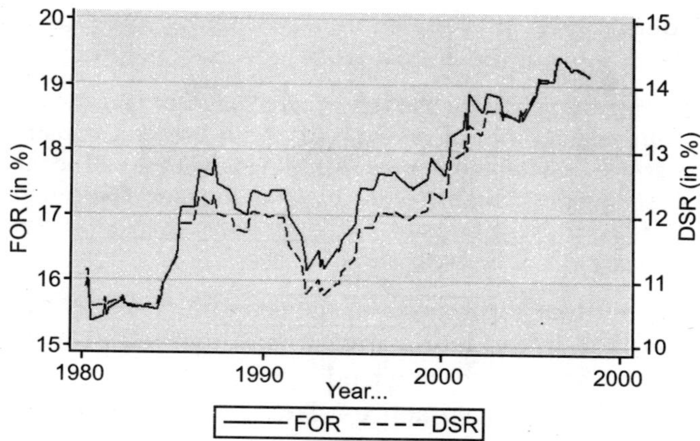

(a) Financial Obligation and Debt Service Ratios

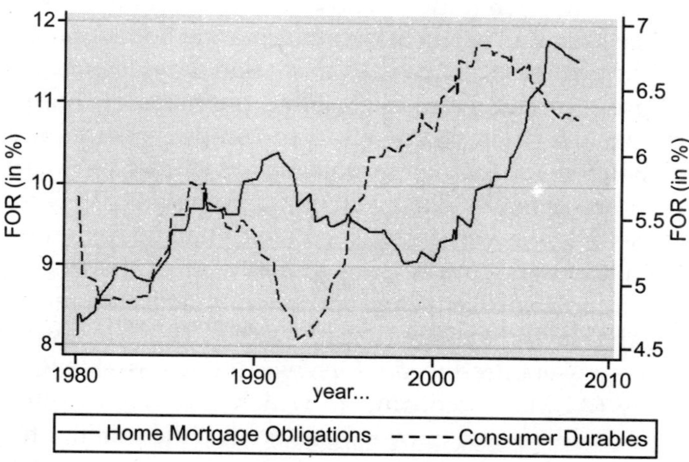

(b) FOR for Home Mortgages and Consumer Durables

Fig. 3. *The Financial Obligation Ratio and Debt Service Ratio for the Household Sector: 1980–2008.1*

FOR for the households.

The Federal Reserve during this period had its priorities chalked out pretty well which was to give a boost to the housing prices, just as in the 90s, it was most interested in maintaining the stock market boom. This can be seen from the minutes of the Federal Open Market Committee (FOMC) meeting of this period. Minutes of the FOMC (2004) meeting held in June say,

> The members continued to report a high level of housing demand in numerous parts of the country, with housing construction described as a notably robust sector in many regional economies. The strong performance of the housing industry continued to be attributed in large measure to the *lowest mortgage interest rates in several decades*. [Emphasis added]

Third, given that the growth of the economy now was driven by the growth in residential investment financed primarily by debt, there was an increasing tendency by the lenders to indulge in predatory lending practices. The norms of lending were broken at will to keep the real estate boom alive and the Fed, despite being aware of the precariousness of the situation, allowed it to happen under its nose just as it did not intervene during the speculative run in the stock market boom of the 90s.

Lending norms were twisted in myriad ways, especially in the subprime mortgage market[4]. First, the norm of mortgage was changed for rich borrowers who could use up to 50 per cent of their income for their mortgage payment whereas earlier the norm was only 28–32 per cent (p. 92, Pollin (2005)). Second, new forms of loans were introduced which had no requirement for down payments. As high as 42 per cent of the first time borrowers and 25 per cent of all borrowers were exempted from making any down payment (Report (2005)). Third, a new form of financing was introduced which was the Adjustable Rate of Mortgage (ARMs), according to which the overall interest payment could be spread over years so that the initial interest payments might seem very low but the debt burden would increase as you go further into future. This was used to sell loans with 'hidden costs'. Fourth, the borrowers could get up to 105 per cent of the buying cost as loan and no documentation of borrower's income or employment was required (Report (2005)). Fifth, the borrowers were allowed to pay only a part of the interest amount due while their unpaid interest amount and the principal get added as debt, a form of loan which has been termed as 'negative amortisation loans'. One third of the total loans in the US in 2002 were either interest-only loans or negative amortisation loans (Report (2005)).

The housing market boom had a logic of its own which was in some ways similar to a stock market boom. Since the housing prices were increasing, it provided a good opportunity to make money at the margin by buying low and selling high, just as in the case of equities. Moreover, increasing prices of houses also increase the net worth of the owners of the houses which further increases their capacity to borrow and hence to speculate even more, which was reflected in people buying more than one house. But since all the buy is financed through debt, it puts the household sector on a knife-edge position. On the one hand, if the prices of the houses declined then the value of their collateral declines and further borrowing becomes less likely. In the worst situation, if the prices fell drastically, even the possibility of repaying the debt by selling the house might itself disappear leading to foreclosures. On the other hand, if the interest rates increase eventually, they would increase the debt burden in future, especially if the loans have been taken under the ARM scheme. In effect, it is the real mortgage rate that matters which is the difference between the nominal mortgage rate and the capital gain through a housing price rise (Weller (2006)).

Even though it was obvious that the housing prices were primarily speculative in nature, Alan Greenspan, the then Chairman of the Federal Reserve, while addressing the Joint Economic Committee on June 9, 2005, had rubbished all claims about the housing boom being a speculative bubble by arguing that,

> [T]here can be little doubt that *exceptionally low interest rates* on ten-year Treasury notes, and hence on home mortgages, have been a major factor in the recent surge of homebuilding and home turnover, and especially in the *steep climb in home prices.* Although a "bubble" in home prices for the nation as a whole does *not* appear likely, there do appear to be, at a minimum, signs of *froth* in some local markets where home prices seem to have risen to unsustainable levels...
>
> Transactions in second homes ... suggest that speculative activity may have had a greater role in generating the recent price increases than it has customarily had in the past.

> The apparent *froth* in housing markets may have spilled over into mortgage markets. The dramatic increases in the prevalence of interest-only loans, as well as the introduction of other relatively exotic forms of adjustable-rate mortgages, are developments of particular concern. To be sure, these financing vehicles have their *appropriate* uses. But to the extent that some households may be employing these instruments to purchase a home that would otherwise be unaffordable, their use is beginning to add to the pressures in the marketplace.
>
> The US economy has weathered such episodes before without experiencing significant declines in the national average level of home prices. In part, this is explained by an underlying uptrend in home prices...
>
> Although we certainly cannot rule out home price declines, especially in some local markets, these declines, were they to occur, likely would *not* have substantial macroeconomic implications. [Emphasis added]

It would be really surprising to note that the same Greenspan had an altogether different take on the Depression of the 1930s. Greenspan (1966) wrote,

> When business in the United States underwent a mild contraction in 1927, the Federal Reserve created more paper reserves in the hope of forestalling any possible bank reserve shortage... *The excess credit which the Fed pumped into the economy spilled over into the stock market-triggering a fantastic speculative boom.* Belatedly, Federal Reserve officials attempted to sop up the excess reserves and finally succeeded in braking the boom. But it was too late: by 1929 the speculative imbalances had become so overwhelming that the attempt precipitated a sharp retrenching and a consequent demoralizing of business confidence. As a result, the American economy collapsed. [Emphasis added]

If we say that 'the excess credit which the Fed pumped into the economy spilled over into the housing market-triggering a fantastic speculative boom', then how different would that be from what his argument is? If not, then it sounds puzzling as to why he did not apply his own argument about the Great Depression to the policy of the Fed under his chairmanship. Whitney (2005) writes the following about the policy of the Fed and its former chairman,

> Greenspan knows all about "irrational exuberance"; he's its primary champion. The Fed seduces the public with cheap money, so that credit spending increases and, then, "presto", millions of Americans slip inexorably into indentured servitude.

Given the delicate balance that the household sector was maintaining vis-à-vis the housing market, it was obvious that any meltdown in these markets would be disastrous not only for the US economy but for the world economy as well. This possibility was further precipitated by the fact that dual pressure fell on the borrowers. On the one hand, the Fed decided to increase the federal fund rate, which increased the interest burdens especially for consumers who had opted for ARMs or negatively amortised loans. On the other hand, decline in housing prices decreased the value of their collateral and thus increased the possibility of bankruptcy which indeed were quite high in this period. This would especially have serious consequences for the US economy, as can be seen today, because 90 per cent of the growth witnessed during 2001-05 was due to increased consumption and residential investment of the households.

Till now we have presented a macroeconomic picture of the housing market but it is obvious that such a market has the potential of having an asymmetric effect on households depending on their income category. For the poorer households, the effect of an increase in the real mortgage rate would be more severe than a richer household.

Some broad pattern can be drawn about the different categories of households (see Table 3). First, the bottom quintile was not a part of the recent run in the housing market since 2001. The value of home as a proportion of income increases the most for the middle quintile. Second, contrary to the general perception, the main customers of ARMs appear to be the richest households and not the poorer ones. This could be because of the fact that the rich were buying the house only for the purposes of selling it later and were financing it through ARMs. A housing market meltdown would, thus, have an asymmetric effect on these categories depending on their relative exposure to the credit market.

Table 3: Financial Condition of the Different Category of Households during the Housing Boom

(% increase)

	Home Value/ Income		*Mortgage Payment/Income*		*Families with ARM*		*ARM/Total Mortgage*		*Houses/ Total Assets*	
Period	*1989-'01*	*2001-'04*	*1989-'01*	*2001-'04*	*1989-'01*	*2001-'04*	*1989-'01*	*2001-'04*	*1989-'01*	*2001-'04*
Total	1.50%	16.7	0.1	0.4	–1.3	1.2	–1.7	2.2	–0.6	1.8
Categories										
Bottom quintile	13.3	6.2	0.9	–0.9	–1.9	-0.2	–2.8	–0.9	0.2	–0.8
Second quintile	2.3	16.5	0.3	1	0	0.4	–0.3	2	0	1.2
Middle quintile	1.4	22.7	0.3	0.4	–1.6	0.1	–2.3	0.2	–0.4	4.1
Fourth quintile	2.5	16.6	0.1	0.7	–1.6	1	–2.1	1.7	–0.4	1.8
Top quintile	-0.2	14.1	0.1	0.3	–1.1	2.7	–1.5	3.2	–0.4	1.7

Source: Weller (2006)

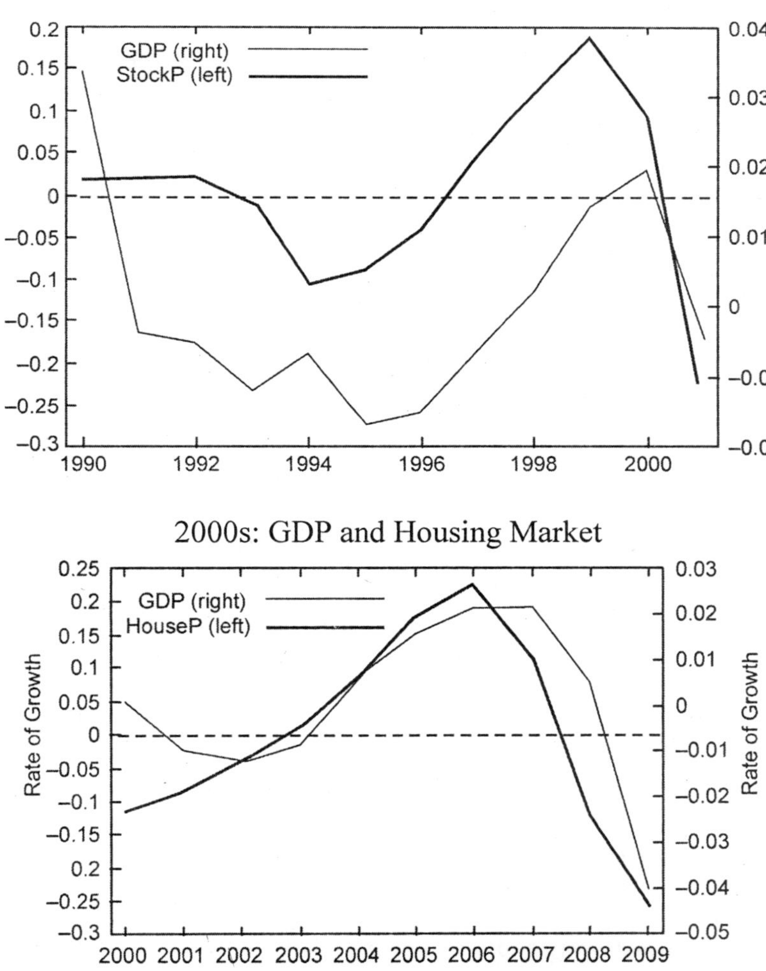

Fig. 4. *Business Cycles and the Asset Price Markets in the 1990s and 2000s*

The fact that the growth process in the last two decades was dependent on asset price markets can be substantiated if we plot the movements in economic activity with respect to these markets. We attempt to plot the business cycle of the 1990s and 2000s against the cycle in the stock market and the housing marker respectively in Figure 4.

It can be seen that in both the cycles the movement of GDP is closely linked to the movement in these markets. In fact, the GDP cycle *follows* the asset price cycles. This gives us some empirical evidence on the theoretical proposition made above. In Keynes' words, the growth processes had become 'bubble in the whirlpool of speculation'.

Is 'It' Over?

A lot is being written about the end of the crisis or at least 'the worst is over'. But we believe, given the magnitude of the crisis, it is premature to think so. When we say the crisis, we do not mean the subprime crisis *per se*. By end of the crisis, we mean the delinking of the growth process' dependence on the speculative booms in the asset price markets. It is very possible that in the short term we have another asset price bubble which will provide some respite to the economy but only to aggravate the systemic problem in the long run.

Let us first examine the economic variables which can tell us about the present recovery process. To examine the extent of recovery, we have to first examine the components of the recovery. Since the US economy is facing a crisis of inadequate aggregate demand in the economy, the path of recovery has to somehow solve this problem. Its failure to do so would not only prolong the crisis but any premature withdrawal of the government stimulus would further aggravate the very problem it is seeking to address. Aggregate demand in any economy comprises of the consumption of the household sector, investment made by the household sector (residential investment), investment made by the corporations (non-residential investment), government expenditure and net exports (trade surplus).

Not only has the residential market plummeted seriously, there has been a decline in the share of consumption too in the present crisis for reasons well known. Together they form a deadly combination of declining investment and the income multiplier. Therefore, the path to recovery has to be dependent on the last three components of aggregate demand, i.e non-residential investment, government expenditure and trade surplus. Let us look at what is happening to these three factors at present (see Figure 5).

Contributors to the Rate of Growth: 2007Q1 to 2009Q3

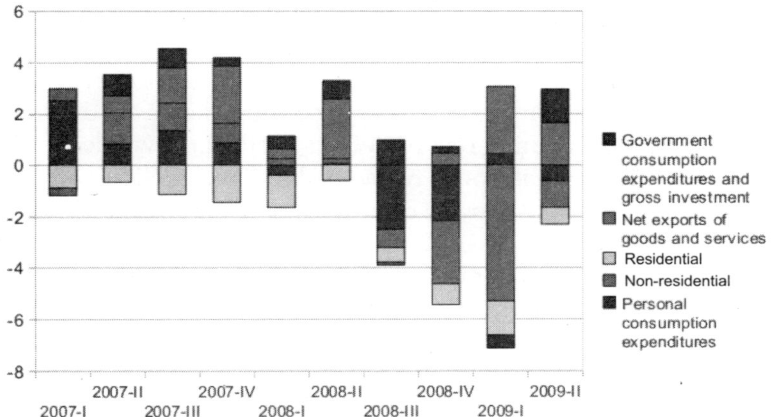

Fig. 5: *What is Driving the US Recovery?*

Non-residential investment or the corporate investment in 'real' capital continues to decline as a proportion of GDP, which itself is serious because it means a lower rate of growth in investment than the GDP. But this is a general trend during the periods of crisis. In any crisis, the first factor that is affected is the corporate investment precisely because of the crisis of confidence of the capitalists. So, this by itself is not novel to this crisis, especially if we see it in the light of the magnitude of the present crisis.

The stimulus package that the Obama administration has injected into the economy has led to increase in the second factor mentioned above, i.e. government expenditure. This automatically has the effect of propping up demand and thus, the GDP. But its magnitude is crucial, especially in crises like these. First, it has to compensate for the decline both in residential and non-residential investment. Second, even if that is taken care of, the net effect of that increase would be dampened if the income multiplier is decreasing as a result of declining share of consumption (as explained above). Therefore, the increase in government expenditure has to take care of both these factors which demands far more than what President Obama has announced so far.

Finally, the third factor, i.e. the trade balance, can also play a role in the recovery. In fact, as we will see below, the most crucial factor contributing to whatever little recovery that the US is witnessing today is directly linked to what is happening in their current account. Though it might seem contrary to common perception that current account balance in the US, which has been running record deficits for the last two decades, could actually be a catalyst to recovery. But if one looks carefully, if the rate of increase of trade deficit is low compared to the rate of decline in growth of GDP, it could actually play a positive role in recovery. In other words, if the 'leakage' of income from the economy in the form of net imports declines during the crisis, it will put less downward pressure on the rate of growth. This is what seems to be happening in the US. The share of trade deficit in the GDP has declined during the period of the crisis giving a positive impetus to an otherwise declining rate of growth.

A decline in the trade deficits could happen if there is an increase in the share of exports in the GDP or a decline in the share of imports or both. Or, at least the decrease in the share of exports in the GDP is lower than that of imports if both are decreasing. Declining trade deficit has taken place during this period in the US due to a sharper rate of decline in imports than exports. Further categorisation of imports reveals that two factors, namely, industrial supplies and materials (except petroleum and products) and automotive vehicles, engines, and parts together have accounted for more than half the decline in imports in these quarters. This nature of decline in the share of imports in the GDP seems more to be of a short term character than a policy response by the US to increasing trade deficits, which makes this component of recovery even for a medium term suspect.

After analysing various components of demand and their behaviour during the 'recovery period', we can say that the increased government expenditure in the US through the fiscal package has still not been able to stimulate the economy to the extent of alleviating the problem at hand. On the one hand, consumption has stagnated, thereby, terminating the route to recovery through an increase in the multiplier. On the other hand, neither the residential investment nor the non-residential investment is showing any sign of recovery, especially, since the level of confidence of the corporations to invest is still quite bleak. Therefore, to withdraw the stimulus package now would be far from prudent. The lessons of the Great Depression remind us that the decision to withdraw the stimulus, on the basis of initial signs of recovery, ended up prolonging the crisis to almost a decade.

Conclusion

We have argued in this paper that growth in the US economy in the recent past has entirely been driven by either consumption spending or residential investment. Both of these were driven by asset price inflation of one kind or the other. While consumption was driven by the stock market boom of the 90s, residential investment was driven by the housing price boom. Such a growth path, however, has serious problems as already being witnessed in the US. First, it would require asset price inflation of one or the other kind to sustain the wealth driven growth. Second, it would be a highly volatile growth path because it would be dependent on the vagaries of these asset price markets. Third, it would invariably force the government to act in the interests of the finance capital because they hold the key to growth in the economy as happened in the bailout package endorsed by the US Congress earlier. The monetary as well as fiscal policy would have to be tethered to the developments in the asset price markets.

The current economic crisis that capitalism is faced with is of far greater magnitude than was envisaged even a few months back precisely because of the extent to which the machinations of the globalised finance capital has spread across the world. This is the time to categorically reject 'there is no alternative' (TINA) paradigm of the neoliberalism and reassert alternative policy prescriptions which would be beneficial to common people.

(August, 2010)

REFERENCES

FOMC (2004): "Meeting of the Federal Open Market Committee," Discussion Paper, Board of the Governors of the Federal Reserve System.

Greenspan, A. (1966): "Gold and Economic Freedom," The Objectivist.

Kalecki, M. (1943): "Political Aspects of Full Employment" in *Selected Essays on the Dynamics of the Capitalist Economy,* Cambridge University Press, 1971.

New York Times Editorial: "Watch This Case", April 16, 2010 available at http://www.nytimes.com/2010/04/17/opinion/17sat2.html?hp, accessed on April 17, 2010.

Piketty, T. and E. Saez (2003): "Income Inequality in the United States, 1913-1998," *Quarterly Journal of Economics*, 118, 1–39.

Pollin, Robert (2005): *Contours of Descent: US Economic Fractures and the Landscape of Global Austerity*. Verso.

Report (2005): "In Come the Waves: The Global Housing Boom," *The Economist*.

Weller, C. E. (2006): "The End of the Great American Housing Boom: What it Means for You, Me and the US Economy," Discussion Paper, Center for American Progress.

Whitney, M. (2005): "Pop Goes the Weasel: Greenspan and the Housing Bubble," *Monthly Review*.

ENDNOTES

1. It is another matter that the nature of state intervention was militarist in nature. Therefore, it would be simplistic to argue that the state intervention was primarily pro-people. In fact, the initial reversal in the economic activity after the prolonged period of Great Depression came after World War II started. This led to increased fiscal expenditure on the part of the government, which pushed the growth up. It is important to note that this growth was purely militaristic in nature. But post-1950s, there was an attempt to prop up the growth and employment by what later came to be known as 'welfare capitalism'. It is of course a contentious issue as to how much of the growth even in this period was welfare-oriented.

2. The argument underlying the negative linkage between growth and inequality can be found even in Marx when he talks about the underconsumption crisis. Josef Steindl, Baran and Sweezy and Kalecki revived this view in the field of Economics.
3. This policy response was best exemplified by Ronald Reagan in the US and Margaret Thatcher in the UK where they proposed small governments to allow free markets to function uninhibitedly. It should be kept in mind, however, that despite the opposition to government intervention in social sectors, they did not have any problems with burgeoning military expenditure. So, the argument effectively was to keep the 'unnecessary' government expenditure under check.
4. With every passing day results of the investigations into the financial sector are getting murkier. A recent example of this is the recent case against the Goldman Sachs (*NY Times* Editorial, April 17, 2010).

   Goldman Sachs Group Inc has been charged with fraud by the US Securities and Exchange Commission over its marketing of a subprime mortgage product. It argued that Goldman Sachs was involved in the malicious practice of creating and selling mortgage-backed investments and then placing financial bets that those investments would fail.

Contributors

Bülent Gökay is Professor of International Studies at Keele University (UK)

Spyros Lapatsioras teaches Economics at the University of Crete (Greece)

Leonidas Maroudas is Associate Professor at the University of the Aegean (Greece)

Panayotis G. Michaelides is Assistant Professor at National Technical University of Athens (Greece)

John Milios is Professor at National Technical University of Athens (Greece)

Anitra Nelson is Associate Professor at RMIT University (Australia)

Michael Perelman is Professor of Economics at California State University (Chico, US)

Rohit is Assistant Professor of Economics at South Asian University (Delhi)

D.P. Sotiropoulos is Lecturer at Kingston University (UK)

Darrell Whitman is a researcher and activist in California (US)